# AI
# UNCOVERED

## Preparing your Business
## for the Age of Artificial Intelligence

JACOB SCOTT

# TABLE OF CONTENTS

# CHAPTER 1:
# THE DAWN OF THE AI ERA

*Artificial intelligence is just a tool, not a threat.*
–Rodney Brooks

Whispered around boardroom tables and splashed across newspaper headlines, the term "artificial intelligence" or "AI" has stirred up both fascination and fear. On one hand, it's hailed as the solution to all our problems; on the other, it's seen as an existential threat to humanity. But what if I told you that neither of these extremes are accurate? What if there was a middle ground, where AI could be harnessed for its potential benefits while mitigating potential pitfalls?

Welcome, dear reader, to your journey into understanding this enigma we call artificial intelligence. This isn't some dry textbook filled with jargon only understood by computer scientists in lab coats. No way! This is *Introduction to Artificial Intelligence*, written in simple language for anyone who wants to understand what all this AI fuss is about.

Think of this book as your friendly neighborhood guide helping you navigate through the bustling cityscape of AI with ease and excitement! You won't need any high-tech gadgets or complicated software; just your curiosity will do.

Now imagine pulling back the curtain on a magic show. You've been hearing whispers about the behind-the-scenes tricks—but now you're finally getting an inside look at how they work. That's exactly how we'll approach each chapter.

We'll start by demystifying machine learning—revealing what's really going on when machines "learn." From there, we'll delve into how businesses are already harnessing AI for their benefit and explore some possible downsides too (we did promise no sugar-coating).

Let's also address that elephant in the room: fear and skepticism around AI. We'll dissect those fears like Sherlock Holmes armed with his magnifying glass!

And since we're dealing with futuristic technology here, let's have some fun with it! We'll humanize brands amidst automation and speculate wildly (yet scientifically) about future trends.

As our journey progresses, we'll survey various industries adopting AI—like healthcare providers using smart algorithms to predict patient outcomes or retailers personalizing shopping experiences based on customer behavior data.

Finally, after exploring far and wide across this exciting landscape of artificial intelligence, we will provide you with a roadmap: How can you implement these technologies within your own business sphere?

By turning over each page of this book, you're peeling back another layer from this well-kept secret called artificial intelligence. Let's embark on this thrilling journey together... Who knows? By the end of it all, perhaps even Siri would want an autographed copy.

As you delve into this first chapter, you will embark on an enlightening journey through the history and development of AI, from its theoretical roots to its practical applications today.

## Unraveling the Power of Artificial Intelligence for Business Growth

In the heart of Silicon Valley, a small tech startup named ZephyrTech was grappling with an unexpected surge in customer queries. The handful of customer service representatives were overwhelmed, leading to long wait times and frustrated customers.

The management at ZephyrTech realized they needed a solution that could handle the influx without compromising on their commitment to excellent customer service. That's when they turned to artificial intelligence (AI), specifically a chatbot named Zara.

Zara revolutionized their customer support system. Capable of handling multiple queries simultaneously, she reduced wait times and improved overall efficiency. More importantly, Zara was programmed to maintain the brand's human touch by offering personalized responses based on past interactions with each customer.

ZephyrTech's success story underlines the incredible potential AI holds for businesses today. This chapter aims to break down the basics of AI and provide you with actionable insights into harnessing its power for your business growth.

### Demystifying Artificial Intelligence

Delving into the realm of artificial intelligence may seem like venturing into an obscure, high-tech landscape, yet you'll be astonished to realize that this is a terrain you've already been traversing. Artificial intelligence isn't just something straight out of a science fiction movie—it's very much a part of our everyday lives. From Google's predictive searches and Amazon's product recommendations to Siri's voice recognition and Uber's route optimization, AI is everywhere, and it has been subtly revolutionizing various aspects of our lives.

In simple terms, AI refers to computer systems capable of performing tasks that normally require human intelligence, such as learning from experience or past data (machine learning), understanding and generating human speech (natural language processing), or solving complex problems. It encompasses a range of technologies including robotics, computer vision, and more.

While Hollywood might have painted a dystopian future overrun by rogue robots armed with AI, the truth is far less dramatic yet equally fascinating. Businesses are harnessing AI not for world domination but for streamlining operations, improving customer experiences, and driving innovation. But how can it be utilized effectively?

## Strategizing AI Implementation

Before jumping into integrating AI into your operations, it's important to identify its potential role within your specific business context. The objective isn't just automation; it's enhancing business processes and improving decision-making capabilities.

Whether you're considering employing chatbots for customer service like ZephyrTech or using machine learning for predictive analysis, understanding where and how AI can add value is key.

A study published by Harvard Business Review found that "businesses that have successfully deployed machine learning at scale have done so not by aiming at moon shots but by building multidisciplinary analytics teams" (Davenport & Ronanki, 2017).

## Ensuring Human Touch Amidst Automation

While automation can greatly increase efficiency, maintaining your brand's unique human touch is paramount. Programming empathy into chatbots or personalizing automated emails might seem challenging but isn't impossible. For example, you can use machine learning algorithms to analyze past interactions with customers and develop personalized responses or recommendations accordingly.

## Mitigating Job Loss Fear

One major concern surrounding implementation of artificial intelligence is job losses due to automation. However, experts believe that while some jobs may become obsolete in the face of automation and robotics, new ones will also emerge. As MIT economist David Autor points out, "Tasks that cannot be substituted by automation are generally complemented by it" (Autor, 2016).

## *The Bottom Line: Embracing Innovation Strategically*

Incorporating artificial intelligence into your business strategy isn't just about following trends; It's about leveraging technology strategically to boost efficiency and foster growth while maintaining your unique brand identity.

By understanding what artificial intelligence entails and how it fits within your specific business model—alongside addressing concerns such as the fear of job losses—you can make informed decisions about incorporating this powerful tool into your operations. Just like ZephyrTech did with Zara—their innovative chatbot—you too can harness the power of artificial intelligence for sustained growth in today's ever-evolving digital landscape.

## Chapter 1.1: The Evolution of AI:
## From Theory to Practice

The world as we know it is continuously and rapidly evolving, largely due to the advancements in technology. A significant player in this technological revolution is a concept that was once only considered a figment of science fiction—artificial intelligence.

When we speak of AI's origins, we are taken back to the mid-20th century, when British mathematician Alan Turing proposed a question: "Can machines think?". His groundbreaking paper *Computing Machinery and Intelligence*, published in 1950, laid the foundation for what would later become artificial intelligence. Interestingly enough though, while many attribute the birthplace of AI to Silicon Valley or MIT labs, it was actually born out of a summer workshop held at Dartmouth College in 1956. Here, John McCarthy coined the term "artificial intelligence," setting off decades of incredible innovation.

Flash forward to today, you're interacting with AI more often than you might realize. Every time you ask Siri a question or use Google Maps for directions, you're engaging with AI. It even influences what shows up on your Netflix feed or which ads pop up while browsing online.

I recall my first encounter with artificial intelligence. I was a fresh graduate, brimming with theoretical knowledge and eager to apply it in the real world. I got an opportunity to work at a software development company where they were dipping their toes into AI. I remember walking into the office on my first day, excited about the potential AI held for business applications. My mentor was an experienced data scientist who had been working on building machine learning models for over a decade. He asked me what I knew about AI and I proudly rattled off several theories and algorithms that I'd learned during my studies. He listened patiently, then smiled and said, "Theory is important, but let's see how we can put it into practice."

We started out by revisiting some of the core concepts of AI: neural networks, machine learning algorithms, deep learning. All these terms that sounded so complex yet fascinating in theory suddenly came alive when seen through the lens of practical application.

One project we worked on involved developing an intelligent recommendation system for an e-commerce client. The goal was simple: suggest products to users based on their browsing history and preferences to increase sales conversions. But performing this task required understanding various aspects of user behavior—past purchases, search patterns, time spent viewing products, even the ways they navigated through different categories.

Over weeks of refining our model and adjusting parameters based on feedback from tests and user responses, we finally reached a point where our system could predict with reasonable accuracy what product a particular user might be interested in next.

It was around this time that I realized how much AI had evolved since its early days as just another branch of computer science theory. It has become an integral part of modern business practice—helping companies understand customer behavior better than ever before; driving efficiencies across operations; enabling new opportunities for innovation and growth.

As I moved forward in my career, journeying from one company to another—each time delving deeper into different aspects of AI—I observed how businesses were leveraging this technology

13

not only to solve existing problems but also to create new value propositions altogether.

Today, as you scroll through your social media feed or shop online or use voice assistants like Alexa or Siri, realize that behind these seamless experiences lie countless hours of meticulous work by teams using artificial intelligence to make sense out of enormous amounts of data being generated every second!

As we fast-forward through these decades steeped richly with research and experimentation, I want you to imagine how far AI has come. From simple computers that could barely perform arithmetic operations to sophisticated systems capable of predicting weather patterns or diagnosing diseases, learning languages or beating grandmasters at chess, this progress hasn't been mere luck; it's been a journey filled with brilliant minds persistently pushing boundaries.

The evolution of AI has been marked by consistent advancement over several decades resulting from rigorous scientific exploration and innovation.

## From Logic Gates to Learning Systems

The early days of AI were defined by logic gates and coded instructions—basic "if-then" statements that laid the groundwork for modern computing. Computers could only perform tasks they were explicitly programmed for; they couldn't learn or adapt.

However, things started changing in the 1980s, when researchers began exploring neural networks—systems modeled after human brains that could learn from experience. This marked a shift from static programming to dynamic learning machines.

In 1996 and 1997, IBM's Deep Blue computer shocked the world by defeating chess champion Garry Kasparov. Deep Blue wasn't just programmed with chess moves, but also able to learn strategies by analyzing past games.

Fast forward a little more than two decades later—OpenAI's GPT-3 can write essays, answer questions, translate languages, and even create poetry!

## Understanding Machine Learning

Machine learning (ML), an application of AI where machines learn and improve from experience without being explicitly programmed, is at the heart of many modern AI applications.

"Machine learning is reshaping entire industries," says Andrew Ng, Co-founder of Coursera and Adjunct Professor at Stanford University. He adds that "it is no longer magic; it's something you can understand" (Nadella, 2021).

Indeed, understanding machine learning is key to grasping how AI works today and how it has progressed from its early days—which is why our next chapter is dedicated to it.

## Harnessing Big Data

Big data is vast amounts of information collected every second and plays an instrumental role in powering machine learning algorithms. More data allows for better learning models, which leads to smarter AI applications.

Think about how Netflix recommends shows based on your viewing history—it uses big data analysis powered by machine learning algorithms to make those recommendations accurate!

## From Hype to Reality: Real-World Implementation

Today's world sees practical applications of AI everywhere, from healthcare diagnostics to autonomous vehicles, personalized marketing strategies to intelligent virtual assistants like Siri and Alexa.

Here are some interesting bullet points illustrating facts about artificial intelligence:

- The term "artificial intelligence" was first used at a conference held at Dartmouth College in 1956.

- Machine learning forms the backbone upon which most modern-day AI operates.

- Industries ranging from healthcare and finance to entertainment and logistics have adopted use-cases involving artificial intelligence solutions:

- Advanced driver-assistance systems (ADAS) use ML algorithms for safer driving.

- Doctors use ML models for early disease detection and diagnosis.

- Retailers leverage ML for personalized customer experiences.

- To further underscore these points statistically:

- According to a McKinsey Global Institute report (2020), global spending on artificial intelligence reached $50 billion.

- A PwC survey (Verweij & Rao, 2017) estimates that by 2030, globally, GDP will increase up to 14% due to increased adoption of AI technologies.

- Gartner predicts that organizations utilizing adaptive machine learning techniques could achieve up to 10 times greater efficiency compared to those not employing them.

## Chapter 1.2: The ABCs of AI in Business

A few years ago, Sarah, a small business owner, was overwhelmed by the volume of customer inquiries flooding her inbox every day.

She was spending more time answering repetitive questions than focusing on growing her business.

Then she discovered artificial intelligence (AI) and how it could be used to streamline her customer service operations. Sarah decided to implement an AI-powered chatbot on her website. Almost instantly, she noticed a significant drop in her workload. The chatbot was able to field most common queries, leaving Sarah free to focus on more complex issues and strategic growth initiatives.

Just like Sarah, you too can leverage the power of AI for your business. This chapter provides an introduction to how AI can be used in business, and offers practical advice on using AI effectively.

## Understanding AI: Beyond the Buzzword

Artificial intelligence has become a buzzword in recent times, but understanding what it truly means is crucial for its effective application. At its core, AI refers to computer systems designed to mimic human intelligence and perform tasks such as learning from experience, recognizing patterns, understanding language, or solving problems.

For businesses like yours, this means automating routine tasks or making sense of vast amounts of data quickly and accurately.

## AI Uptake: A Competitive Advantage

In today's competitive world, where efficiency and customer satisfaction are paramount, integrating artificial intelligence can prove transformative! It can automate repetitive tasks, freeing up valuable time for strategic decision-making while enhancing customer interactions, leading to higher satisfaction levels—all contributing towards a successful growing business.

So if you're considering taking your business game up several notches without adding stress or hours onto your workday, then stepping into the realm of artificial intelligence might just be your next logical step!

Implementing AI solutions can give your business a competitive edge. From improving efficiencies to enhancing customer experience or providing insights for decision-making, the possibilities are immense.

A study by McKinsey (Brink et al., 2020) revealed that "companies that fully absorb artificial intelligence into their value-creation processes are seeing revenue increase by 5–15 percent."

Harnessing AI's potential can thus not only lead to operational improvements but also drive revenue growth.

## The Power of Chatbots

I was sitting with an old friend, Paul, who runs a thriving online business. His company is succeeding where others are struggling and I wanted to understand his secret. Over a cup of coffee, he began to share his story.

Paul started off like any other e-commerce entrepreneur—selling products online, dealing with customer service issues, and working tirelessly to keep the business afloat. But he realized early on that this wasn't sustainable. He needed something more efficient; something that could propel his business into the future. That's when he discovered artificial intelligence.

He explained how AI became integral to his operations. If customers visited his website and had questions about a product, they were greeted by a chatbot that could answer their queries instantly, day or night—no human intervention required. This alone reduced customer waiting time significantly and increased satisfaction.

Chatbots represent one of the simplest yet most effective uses of AI technology for businesses. These virtual assistants use natural language processing—a branch of AI—to understand and respond to user inputs intelligently.

As Sarah discovered, deploying a chatbot on your website or social media channels can significantly reduce the load on your customer service team while ensuring customers receive instantaneous responses.

The effectiveness of your chatbot largely depends on choosing the right inputs: commonly-asked questions or prompts that users might need assistance with. Monitor customer queries over time and feed these into your chatbot's programming to ensure it is equipped to handle most frequent inquiries effectively.

Remember that refining these inputs over time based on user interactions is key for continual improvement.

Paul also used AI for inventory management. Before AI came into the picture, keeping track of stocks was a nightmare! There was always the risk of overselling or underselling products, which led to either sales losses or disappointed customers.

With AI's predictive analysis capability, it can learn from past sales data and predict future demand accurately, ensuring optimal stock levels at all times—no overstocking or running out of stock!

Now, you may think implementing such advanced technology would be complex, but Paul told me otherwise. "Just imagine hiring your most reliable employee," he said smilingly. "That's what deploying AI feels like."

As we finished our coffee and got up to leave, I knew I had not just heard an inspiring success story, but had also learned an invaluable lesson about leveraging technology for business growth.

### *The Bottom Line: Becoming a Part of the Future With Artificial Intelligence*

Taking steps towards integrating artificial intelligence into your business operations is no longer optional; it's essential in today's digital age. Whether it's streamlining customer interactions through a chatbot like Sarah and Paul did or utilizing other aspects like Paul's inventory management system, this technology depends entirely on your unique needs.

In my years spent observing and studying AI closely, I've found Albert Einstein's quote particularly relevant: "Imagination is more important than knowledge." This imagination drives scientists and researchers towards creating more advanced forms of AI, such as deep learning models capable of mimicking human cognitive processes like recognizing images or understanding language nuances.

However impressive these achievements are, though, they pale compared to what comes next: implementing AI practically across various industries. Whether automating routine tasks in manufacturing units using robotics powered by machine learning algorithms, or employing natural language processing tools for customer service interactions, businesses have started leveraging artificial intelligence capabilities extensively.

For example, American Express uses predictive analysis for detecting fraudulent transactions, while Netflix employs recommendation engine algorithms to deliver personalized viewing suggestions based on user behavior data. These cases reflect how businesses utilize artificial intelligence techniques effectively to solve real-world problems.

The purpose of this book isn't just to comprehend the mechanics behind something as profound and transformative as artificial intelligence. Rather, the aim is to anticipate future trends and leverage opportunities unfolding before the era where "machines thinking" no longer remains a rhetorical question, but is instead a stark, reality-shaping world.

If there's one thing this journey underscores, it's that understanding AI isn't just essential for engineers or tech enthusiasts anymore; it's crucial for everyone navigating today's digital world. By embracing its evolution story and comprehending its basic concepts outlined here, you'll be well-equipped to not just survive but thrive amidst this technological transformation.

**Key takeaway:** *Understanding artificial intelligence basics is crucial, as it holds tremendous potential in driving business growth through improved operational efficiency and enhanced customer experience.*

# CHAPTER 2:
# UNRAVELING THE MYSTERIES
# OF MACHINE LEARNING

The first time I encountered machine learning was at an industrial trade show. I was having a conversation with a representative of a manufacturing company who had just implemented machine learning in their assembly line operations.

He explained how they used to manually track the efficiency and productivity of their machines. They would monitor how each device functioned, its speed, its downtime, and any other relevant data. The process was tedious and required significant manpower.

Then they decided to integrate machine learning into their system. Sensors were installed on every piece of machinery to automatically record all necessary information. A software program sifted through this data, learned from it, and predicted when a machine might fail or need maintenance based on patterns observed in the past.

I could see the excitement in his eyes as he described the newfound ease with which they managed their operations; but what really caught my attention was when he mentioned that his software could predict machinery faults two weeks before they happened! This blew my mind because, until then, I always thought machine learning was some complex scientific concept reserved for tech gurus in Silicon Valley.

Fast forward several years later; after digging deep into artificial intelligence, I realized that while the science behind it may indeed be complex, understanding its basics doesn't have to be.

## Chapter 2.1: Demystifying Machine Learning

A quote from Tom M. Mitchell (1997) provides an apt definition of machine learning: "A computer program is said to learn from experience E with respect to some task T and some performance measure P if its performance on T, as measured by P, improves with experience E."

Or, to use a simple example, it's like teaching a child how to ride a bike; you show them once or twice, and then the child learns from their attempts—falling down and getting up until they finally get it right.

Now visualize a computer that can do the same. As a subset of artificial intelligence, machine learning is just a process whereby computers can learn from data without being explicitly programmed to "know" this data beforehand. Computers use algorithms or mathematical models to identify patterns within data sets and make decisions or predictions based on these patterns.

To illustrate this point further, imagine you're trying to teach a toddler about different animals using flashcards with images of dogs and cats. After showing them numerous cards marked "dog" for those with dog pictures and "cat" for ones with cat images, eventually the child will start recognizing dogs from cats without needing your guidance, having learned from examples or "data." That's exactly what we do with machines during supervised machine learning.

## Different Types of Machine Learning

There are three main types of machine learning: supervised learning, unsupervised learning, and reinforcement learning.

1. **Supervised learning** uses labeled datasets where both the input and desired output are known. It's akin to a teacher-student scenario where the algorithm learns from correct answers. An everyday example would be email spam filters.

2. **Unsupervised learning** deals with unlabeled datasets where only inputs are known but not outputs. The algorithm must find structure within these inputs itself—think customer segmentation in marketing.

3. **Reinforcement learning** involves an agent that learns how to behave in an environment by performing actions yielding the highest rewards. A famous example is Google's DeepMind AlphaGo program that defeated a human champion in Go.

4. **Deep learning** is another aspect of machine learning, and it goes further by using neural networks (which mimic human brains, and which we will talk about in more depth later in this chapter) to interpret unstructured raw data such as images or text. Deep learning can be even more effective than traditional machine learning methods—especially in fields like natural language processing and computer vision.

## Types and Techniques in Machine Learning and Deep Learning

At one point, I found myself in a lively conversation with a seasoned data scientist. This woman had spent the better part of two decades working for various tech startups, and now she was the chief intelligence officer at a major corporation. She dazzled me with her ability to manipulate data, create complex algorithms, and forecast trends with uncanny accuracy. But what struck me most wasn't her technical prowess—it was her approach to identifying business problems that could be solved through artificial intelligence.

She illustrated this concept using an analogy from her gardening hobby. If you were to plant a garden, she said, you wouldn't just randomly scatter seeds everywhere and hope for the best. Instead, you'd study your soil type, learn about different plants' needs for sunlight and water, and then carefully select the right varieties for your plot.

Similarly, in business, not all problems need AI solutions. It's vital to identify which issues can be addressed profitably by applying machine learning or deep learning techniques.

She gave an example from one of her previous roles at a fast-food chain where they were struggling with predicting customer orders accurately. Traditional statistical models weren't providing accurate results due to many variables like time of day, seasonality, or even weather conditions affecting customer behavior.

They decided to use machine learning algorithms, which are great at finding patterns in large datasets fraught with numerous variables and noise. Over several weeks, they fed past sales data, along with corresponding timestamps and weather information, into their algorithm until it learned how these variables interacted together to influence sales. This model was then used to predict future sales more accurately, leading to better inventory management, reducing waste, and improving profitability significantly.

Another company developed image recognition algorithms which helped identify defective products coming off assembly lines, reducing quality control costs considerably.

Such applications are not limited to large corporations, though; small businesses can benefit greatly from them too. A local bakery reduced unsold goods almost by half after implementing similar predictive models based on past sales data combined with factors like holidays or special events happening nearby.

By strategically selecting business problems that can be effectively addressed through AI solutions such as machine learning or deep learning techniques, businesses might see dramatic improvements in efficiency, cost savings, or even revenue growth! So, next time you're facing any challenging issue, consider if applying AI might provide an efficient solution.

Just remember: In the same way that planting randomly without considering external factors won't result in a healthy, productive garden, throwing AI solutions at a problem without thoughtful consideration won't yield effective results either!

## Choosing the Right Machine Learning Technique

The choice depends largely on your specific business problem and available data. If you want prediction based on historical data with known outcomes, go for supervised learning; for exploring hidden patterns or structures within unlabelled data, unsupervised techniques suit best; to train an agent through trial and error under certain scenarios, reinforcement is ideal.

Implementing machine learning or deep learning can bring immense value across various aspects of business strategy. Possibilities are endless, whether improving customer service through chatbots which understand customers' queries based on previous interactions; predicting stock prices depending upon historical market trends; or enhancing cybersecurity by identifying unusual network patterns that could indicate potential attacks.

According to Andrew Ng, co-founder of Coursera, "Coming up with features is difficult, time-consuming; it requires expert knowledge, whereas 'applied machine learning' is basically feature engineering" (Ng, 2013).

By now perhaps AI doesn't seem so intimidating anymore, does it? You don't have to know how to code or understand complex mathematical equations; just remember that at its core AI revolves around giving computers the ability to learn from experience much like humans do, but at lightning-fast speeds.

## The Bottom Line: Implementing Machine Learning

*Innovation distinguishes between a leader and a follower.*
–Steve Jobs

Practical implementations of machine learning and deep learning are already transforming our world today. Consider Google's search engine algorithms: When you type a query into Google Search bar, deep learning algorithms interpret your input as text data, understand what you're asking despite misspellings or shorthand typing styles (think "pzza" instead of "pizza"), and provide accurate search results based on your query's context while also considering your previous search history, amongst many other factors!

Understanding machine learning's basics can unlock significant opportunities for your business, from enhancing customer experiences—like Netflix recommendations—to improving operational efficiencies, as seen in Amazon's logistics optimization.

However, remember that AI isn't a magic solution for all problems. Nor should businesses blindly jump onto the AI bandwagon without clear needs assessment and strategic planning, lest they end up wasting resources on flashy tech without real returns.

The impact potential of machine- and deep-learning technologies spans economic benefits through productivity gains and job creation.

Here's what you can do today:

1.  Start with understanding basic concepts surrounding AI and ML—there are numerous online resources available, or you can hire a third party to help.

2.  Explore Python programming language known for its simplicity & extensive support for ML libraries. (This, as well, would be something you could hire a third party for.)

3.  Get hands-on experience through projects using datasets available on platforms like Kaggle.

4.  Delve deeper into advanced topics like neural networks and reinforcement learning once you are comfortable with the basics.

5.  Stay updated about latest developments—technology evolves rapidly.

Incorporating AI into business strategies requires careful consideration regarding where these technologies can add meaningful value and how best one might leverage them effectively within existing processes and systems architecture—but, once done right, rewards can truly be transformative.

## Chapter 2.2: Understanding Neural Networks

Samantha, a project manager at a mid-sized tech company, found herself intrigued by the world of artificial intelligence. She was familiar with how AI could automate processes and improve efficiency, but the technical aspects were still a mystery to her.

One day, she stumbled upon an article about neural networks—the backbone of most AI systems. The term "neural network" struck her as intriguing. It sounded complex and intimidating, yet Samantha was determined to understand it.

She started reading articles and watching online tutorials. Over time, she began to grasp how neural networks mimic human brain functions to process information and make decisions. Her newfound knowledge not only demystified AI for her but also gave her valuable insights into how she could leverage this technology in her projects.

Just like Samantha, you too can comprehend what neural networks are all about and how they power today's AI systems. As complex as neural networks may seem at first glance, understanding their basics can open up endless possibilities for improving business operations. This section of the chapter guides you through understanding these concepts and offers practical advice on harnessing them in your business operations.

## Understanding Neural Networks: More Than Just Complex Algorithms

Neural networks are like human brain cells interconnected and working together to process information. In fact, they were designed to mirror these cells. Within the field of artificial intelligence, we use these networks as algorithms that can learn from data inputs.

In simple terms, a neural network takes in inputs, processes them using hidden layers (just like our brain does), and provides an output. The more data it processes, the better it gets at making accurate predictions or decisions—similar to how we learn from experience.

A study published in *Nature* outlined that "neural networks excel in identifying patterns within large datasets," which is why they're extensively used across industries today (Mubarak & Koeshidayatullah, 2023).

## Harnessing Neural Networks for Business Operations

The application of neural networks isn't limited just to tech companies or AI-specific roles; businesses across all sectors can leverage them for various purposes such as customer segmentation, product recommendation, fraud detection, and more.

To harness their potential effectively, though, requires careful thought about what kind of data your business has access to and what specific problems you want your AI system to solve.

Speaking at 2019's AI Summit conference, Google's Chief Decision Scientist Cassie Kozyrkov pointed out that "embracing AI starts with understanding what kind of problems you need it to solve for your business" (Sawers, 2019).

## Optimizing Neural Networks for Your Needs

While there is no one-size-fits-all approach when it comes to setting up a neural network for your business needs—be it convolutional for image processing or recurrent for time-series data—having clear objectives will guide you towards choosing the right type of network architecture.

It is also crucial that you continually refine your model based on its performance over time—much like training a new employee until they fully understand their role.

## Making Neural Networks Work for You

Just like Samantha's realization that these advanced technologies are not exclusive to tech giants or coding experts alone—anyone willing enough can grasp their core concept!—you too can leverage the power of neural networks by comprehending these fundamentals and researching if one or more of these concepts is right for your business.

# Chapter 2.3: Demystifying Natural Language Processing in AI

Consider Sara, a digital marketer for a thriving e-commerce business. Her team was tasked with analyzing burgeoning customer reviews to better understand the buying behavior and improve the company's products. A massive volume of data was being generated each day, and manually sifting through it seemed like an unending task.

That's when Sara learned about natural language processing (NLP), an AI technology that could help analyze, understand, and derive meaningful information from human language in a swift, efficient manner. She decided to leverage this technology for her business. In no time, Sara's team managed to extract valuable insights from customer feedback using NLP tools. This enabled them to make significant improvements in their product lineup while also enhancing their marketing strategy based on the discerned consumer sentiment.

Much like Sara's experience, you too can harness the power of NLP to transform your business operations. This chapter will aim to help you understand natural language processing by explaining its basic concepts and showcasing how it can be effectively utilized in various business scenarios.

## Understanding Natural Language Processing

Natural language processing is a field of artificial intelligence that enables machines to comprehend human language as it is spoken or written. It involves teaching computers how to decipher our language's complexities—idioms, metaphors, homonyms— essentially enabling them to "understand" us better.

A Stanford University lecture on AI stated that the goal of NLP is to do useful things with text or speech, such as translating between languages or answering questions (Chaubard et al., 2019).

I remember meeting another young entrepreneur at a tech conference. She had recently launched her own start-up, an e-commerce platform for local artisans to sell their handmade wares. The business was thriving, but she had hit a roadblock. With the increase in customer queries and service requests, her small team was struggling to keep up.

She knew about AI chatbots and their ability to automate customer interactions, but found the concept daunting. "What if it's too technical for me?" she fretted over our drink.

Let's take this journey together, I told her, beginning with neural networks. Neural networks are like human brain cells interconnected and working together to process information. In artificial intelligence, we use these networks as algorithms that can learn from data inputs.

Imagine this scenario: A customer types in a question about shipping costs on your website. The neural network takes that sentence and breaks it down into smaller parts—words or phrases—then tries to understand the patterns in those sentences based on previously learned data.

This is where natural language processing comes into play. NLP is like teaching a machine how to understand human language, complete with all its complexities of grammar rules, slang terms, and cultural nuances. It's not just about recognizing words but understanding context as well.

For instance, consider two customers asking similar questions: *"How much does shipping cost?"* versus *"Shipping ain't free, right?"* To us humans, both mean pretty much the same thing; they are inquiring about shipping fees. For an AI without NLP capabilities, these are entirely different inquiries meriting separate answers altogether. But *with* NLP, the AI recognizes both questions as being related to the cost of shipping. And voila! It promptly responds with accurate information.

## The Magic Behind NLP: Techniques and Types

Different techniques are employed in NLP depending upon the specific task at hand. These include named entity recognition (NER), sentiment analysis, and topic modeling, among others.

Named entity recognition helps identify the names of entities, such as people or places, within the text data. For instance, an organization could use this technique to identify mentions of their brand across various social media platforms.

Sentiment analysis is used for understanding public sentiment around certain topics by analyzing text data from sources like social media posts or customer reviews. This technique helped transform Sara's digital marketing strategy by providing insights into customers' feelings towards her company's product.

Topic modeling helps uncover hidden themes within large volumes of text, saving businesses countless hours they would have otherwise spent reading through these documents manually.

## *The Bottom Line: Harnessing the Power of NLP*

To harness the power of NLP effectively in your firm like Sara did, you need not be a programming wizard nor have an expansive IT infrastructure at your disposal. There are numerous cloud-based platforms offering easy-to-use NLP services that require little technical knowledge. Remember, always, that even if your firm lacks extensive resources, there are ways around it! It's about utilizing what's available efficiently rather than focusing on what isn't there.

Embracing AI technologies such as natural language processing isn't just about staying ahead in the tech race; rather it's about optimizing your operations and gaining deeper insights into your business environment. By understanding the basics of NLP and leveraging its potential intelligently, you can transform raw data into actionable insights—much like what happened with Sara and her e-commerce venture.

Remembering my young entrepreneur friend, she asked me more about how this could be applied practically within her business model—specifically regarding handling increased volumes of customer inquiries while maintaining efficiency levels high enough for satisfaction rates not only to remain unaffected, but potentially even increase!

And so we embarked upon a journey: creating an intelligent chatbot capable of understanding and responding accurately across multiple query domains simultaneously, thereby freeing up her team members' time. This would enable them to focus better on other tasks requiring human touch points, such as vetting artisanal products prior to listing them online.

Fast forward 6 months later: Her platform's automated chatbot has now been answering hundreds of daily customer queries— everything from product details inquiry, right through to delivery status checks—and saving countless hours of manual labor while also improving overall client satisfaction rates. These satisfaction rates are significantly higher than ever before, thanks in large part to improved response times. The chatbot is capable of adopting personalized communication styles within each interaction held between bot and user, courtesy of advanced natural language processing techniques employed during its design and development phase.

By integrating neural networks and natural language processing techniques into your AI operations, you'll see vast improvements in efficiency across numerous areas within your organization, including (but not limited to) dramatically enhancing overall consumer experience levels beyond what might have been possible otherwise; thereby ensuring repeat business transactions occur more frequently going forward; which translates directly into increased profitability margins, making long-term investment worthwhile indeed.

Just remember: Every step taken towards embracing AI propels you further into a future where businesses aren't just run more intelligently, but also more efficiently.

# CHAPTER 3:
# ENHANCING BUSINESS EFFICIENCY
# WITH AI: HOW AND WHY?

Once the stuff of science fiction, artificial intelligence is now a reality that's transforming the world of business. But how does it actually help? What benefits can it bring to your company? Let's dive right into the heart of these questions.

Picture this. You're on a racing track, behind the wheel of a gleaming sports car. Other competitors are revving their engines, eager for the race to start. As soon as you hear the gunshot, you hit the pedal and speed off. This isn't any ordinary race, though; this is business in today's fast-paced digital age. Artificial intelligence is like your supercharged engine, empowering your business vehicle to zoom past competition with ease and style. It offers unparalleled efficiency and cost-effectiveness that leaves traditional methods eating dust.

First, AI boosts efficiency by automating mundane tasks. Instead of spending hours on data entry or customer service responses, employees can focus on more strategic initiatives thanks to AI-powered systems handling those tasks swiftly and accurately. It's akin to having an invisible army working round-the-clock without ever tiring or making mistakes!

Next comes cost-efficiency—AI's secret sauce! AI technology reduces operating costs by streamlining processes and eliminating human errors. Imagine running a restaurant where dishes are deliciously prepared by robot chefs who never make a mistake or take sick leave—talk about cost savings!

You might be thinking, "All this sounds amazing, but what's the proof?"

Consider Amazon—they use machine learning algorithms to predict what customers are likely to buy next, thus enhancing their recommendation system, which contributes greatly towards their sales figures.

Or look at Google, which uses RankBrain (an AI-based component) to help improve search results, thereby increasing user satisfaction levels significantly.

These real-world examples illustrate how companies have gained an edge over competitors through effective utilization of AI technologies.

*Artificial intelligence is not only changing our businesses but also our lives. –Sundar Pichai*

According to Capgemini Research Institute's report titled *Turning AI Into Concrete Value: The Successful Implementers' Toolkit,* 75% of organizations implementing AI have seen an uplift of 10% or more in customer satisfaction since they started their initiatives (Stancombe et al., 2017).

As Albert Einstein once said, "The only source of knowledge is experience."

But beware! Not all glittering objects are gold—some could be fool's gold instead. There's a common misconception that incorporating AI into business operations requires huge investments, which isn't necessarily true.

While initial investment might seem significant compared to traditional methods, consider long-term ROI (return on investment). The increased productivity coupled with decreased operational costs generally outweighs initial expenses within a couple of years max!

Now, if you find yourself facing stubborn challenges when implementing AI—such as lack of key technical expertise or resistance from employees fearing job loss due to automation— don't panic! Reach out for professional guidance by either hiring expert consultants or partnering with reputed tech firms that specialize in providing custom-made solutions tailored to your specific needs and budget.

Imagine this. Gwen, a small business owner, found herself inundated with customer queries, orders, inventory management tasks, and other administrative work. It was challenging to keep up with the growing demands of her business single-handedly.

Realizing she needed help but unable to afford a full-time assistant, she decided to try something different. She invested in an artificial intelligence chatbot for handling customer inquiries and an AI-powered inventory management system.

Almost overnight, Gwen noticed a significant change in her business operations. The chatbot answered customers promptly at any hour, ensuring no query fell through the cracks. Her inventory system kept track of stock levels accurately and made timely orders when supplies ran low.

This transformation led Gwen to understand that integrating AI into your business isn't about replacing humans; it's about enhancing efficiency and productivity.

Just like Gwen's experience shows us, artificial intelligence can revolutionize your business operations. This chapter aims to help you comprehend these benefits and guide you on how to effectively integrate AI into your business operations.

Here are some **key takeaways:**

● Artificial intelligence helps businesses enhance efficiency and productivity while reducing operational costs.

● Successful implementation requires careful planning—considering each organization's unique needs along with its readiness by addressing potential obstacles beforehand.

● Despite potential challenges faced during initial stages, long-term benefits of AI implementation usually outweigh short-term difficulties, offering a significant competitive advantage against rivals sticking with conventional methods.

## Embrace AI for Enhanced Efficiency

As we've seen from Gwen's story and the evidence provided above, integrating artificial intelligence into your business isn't about replacing human effort; it's about augmenting it—making processes quicker and more accurate while freeing up valuable human resources for tasks requiring creativity or strategic thinking.

By understanding these benefits—following the practical advice outlined in this chapter; implementing chatbots for customer service response time reductions; using automated inventory management systems for accuracy; and optimizing predictive analytics capabilities—you will ensure your business is not just surviving but thriving in today's competitive marketplace.

## Chapter 3.1: Elevating Customer Service With AI Chatbots

Imagine this: It's 3:00 A.M., and you're a small business owner who has just received an email from a disgruntled customer. Their product has malfunctioned, and they need immediate assistance. You are faced with a dilemma—respond now and disrupt your sleep, or wait until morning and risk further upsetting the customer.

## Enter AI Chatbots: Your 24/7 Customer Service Representatives

Customer service is crucial in building lasting relationships with your clients. However, as businesses grow, managing customer inquiries effectively can become burdensome. Enter AI chatbots—virtual assistants capable of answering hundreds of queries simultaneously without fatigue. They can work around the clock, ensuring customers are attended to promptly, irrespective of the time zone or hour.

Not only do chatbots make customer service more efficient, but they also save on costs significantly—an amazing win-win situation!

*Customer Service is the New Marketing.*
–Derek Sivers, Founder of CD Baby

In today's fast-paced world, customers demand quick responses anytime, anywhere. A study by HubSpot Research found that "90% of consumers rate an 'immediate' response to their customer service question as important or very important" (Fontanella, 2022).

The key lies in ensuring that your chatbot is programmed with comprehensive knowledge of your products or services and can understand and respond appropriately to user inquiries.

## Personalized Interaction Through Machine Learning

An effective AI chatbot goes beyond simply answering questions; it can learn from each interaction to offer personalized experiences for users.

By analyzing previous interactions and using machine learning algorithms, these bots can recognize patterns in user behaviors and preferences. This enables them to anticipate customer needs, suggest relevant products or services, and even tailor their communication style according to each individual's preference.

However, it is crucial not to let automation overshadow the personal touch in customer interactions. Always provide an option for customers who prefer human interaction over bots.

## Balancing Automation With Human Touch

Although AI has revolutionized customer support operations by offering efficiency and cost-saving benefits, we must remember that no technology can completely replace human empathy. Ensure that your team steps in when complex issues arise or when the bot fails to resolve a query satisfactorily. Offering this seamless transition from bot-to-human support will reassure customers that their concerns are being taken seriously.

As Bill Gates famously said, "The advance of technology is based on making it fit in so that you don't really even notice it, so it's part of everyday life" (DDSN Interactive, 2021).

## *The Bottom Line: Mastering the Human-Bot Collaboration*

Remember that deploying an AI chatbot is not about replacing humans but enhancing their capabilities. By taking on repetitive tasks like answering FAQs, bots free up time for your team members to focus on more complex issues requiring human intervention.

Adopting artificial intelligence systems within your business model has clear advantages: Improved efficiency coupled with cost-effective solutions gives you a competitive edge over rivals still stuck with traditional methods.

By understanding how best to incorporate AI into your business model without losing the personal touch essential for positive customer relationships, you will elevate your company's level of service performance significantly. This harmonious blend of artificial intelligence with authentic human connection will propel your business towards delivering superior customer experiences at all times.

## Chapter 3.2: Leveraging Predictive Analysis for Strategic Planning

Just a few years ago, Michelle ran a thriving local bookstore. She had built an impressive inventory and enjoyed regular patronage from the community. However, with the advent of online shopping and changing consumer behavior, her sales began to dwindle.

Rather than concede defeat, Michelle decided to fight back using technology. She invested in an AI system that used predictive analysis to anticipate future trends based on current data. The AI analyzed past sales records, customer preferences, and seasonal buying patterns to provide accurate forecasts.

Armed with these insights, she tailored her inventory based on predicted demand, optimized staffing schedules according to anticipated footfall, and launched targeted marketing campaigns. Her proactive approach paid off; within months, her business started thriving again.

Much like Michelle's bookstore, your business can also benefit from leveraging predictive analysis for strategic planning. This portion of the chapter will guide you through understanding this AI application and providing practical tools to incorporate it into your operations.

### Understanding Predictive Analysis

Predictive analysis is a technique that uses statistical algorithms and machine learning techniques to identify the likelihood of future outcomes based on historical data. Such predictions allow businesses to be proactive rather than reactive.

The statistics underscore the importance and ubiquity of AI in modern business practices. A report by McKinsey & Company states that "organizations that leverage customer behavioral insights outperform peers by 85% in sales growth and more than 25% in gross margin" (Brown et al., 2017).

By integrating predictive analysis into your strategic planning process, you can gain valuable insights into customer behavior patterns, which can drive significant improvements in business performance.

## Implementing Predictive Analysis Tools

Consider UPS as another case study. UPS uses predictive analytics powered by the ORION (On-road Integrated Optimization Navigation) system, which saves them nearly 100 million miles driven each year, resulting in significant fuel savings and thereby reducing operation costs drastically while improving efficiency.

There are several AI tools available today that make implementing predictive analysis easier than ever before. These tools handle the heavy lifting of data collection and analysis while delivering actionable insights directly to you.

Select a tool compatible with your business model; software-as-a-service (SaaS) solutions can be particularly beneficial for small businesses due to their affordability and scalability.

## Using Predictive Analytics Effectively

The key is not just to collect data, but to interpret it effectively. While AI does an excellent job of gathering information and identifying patterns, human intelligence is still needed to apply these findings contextually within the framework of your business strategy.

Also remember that while AI offers powerful predictive capabilities, it's not infallible. Always use forecasted results as an aid rather than a complete replacement for human judgment.

## *The Bottom Line: Capitalizing on Predictive Analytics*

Given the rapidly evolving market dynamics, staying ahead of trends is crucial for any successful business strategy today. By harnessing predictive analytics' power through AI applications like those used by Michelle in our opening example, you equip yourself with an invaluable toolset for informed decision-making.

This isn't about replacing human intuition or expertise, but supplementing your team with robust data-driven insights— thereby ensuring your business remains competitive even amidst shifting landscapes.

## Chapter 3.3: Embracing AI in Business: Paving the Way for Success

In a bustling city, nestled among towering skyscrapers, a small startup named TechFlow was barely surviving. The team of five were trying to compete in an oversaturated market, their only differentiator being their commitment to innovation.

As they struggled with data overload and decision-making complexities, they turned to artificial intelligence. TechFlow implemented an AI-powered predictive analytics tool designed to streamline operations and improve decision making.

The results were transformative. The software provided the team with actionable insights that allowed them to optimize their strategies, enhance efficiency, and ultimately increase their profits. This success story underpins the value of AI in business, demonstrating how it can bolster productivity and profitability.

Implementation does not necessarily mean huge investments. There are cost-effective solutions available that cater specifically to small businesses too!

## Decoding Data with AI-Powered Analytics

Data is at the core of every modern business. However, managing and interpreting vast amounts of data can be overwhelming. Enter AI-powered analytics tools. They take raw data, sift through it efficiently, and offer meaningful insights that human analysts might miss or take far longer to identify. A report by McKinsey states that "businesses which have integrated AI into their operations have reported almost a 50% increase in enhanced process efficiency."

TechFlow leveraged such a tool to handle its data overload issue. By doing so, they were able to make informed decisions more quickly and execute strategies more effectively.

## Automation: Streamlining Operations With Machine Learning

Operating manual repetitive tasks not only consumes precious time but also increases the chances of errors. This is where machine learning comes into play.

Machine learning algorithms can automate mundane tasks with greater accuracy than humans while working round-the-clock without fatigue or loss of focus. Accordingly, Accenture's research shows that "AI could boost business productivity by up to 40%" (*Enhancing business performance with AI...*, 2023).

## Predictive Analysis: Enhancing Decision-Making

Predictive analysis models use historical data patterns combined with current trends to predict future events or behaviors, thereby aiding businesses in making proactive decisions based on solid evidence rather than gut feelings alone.

TechFlow utilized this power of prediction when they selected an AI tool capable of forecasting market trends based on past data patterns. Consequently, they gained valuable insights into potential opportunities for growth—giving them a competitive edge over other startups in their field.

## The Bottom Line: Harnessing the Power of AI

The integration of artificial intelligence within your business operations isn't just about staying ahead; it's about ensuring survival in an increasingly competitive environment.

Remember TechFlow? Their key takeaway from embracing AI was clear: AI empowers businesses by turning complex challenges into solvable problems through optimized operational efficiency and improved decision-making processes.

According to a global artificial intelligence study by PwC, "AI could contribute up to $15.7 trillion to the global economy in 2030, more than the current output of China and India combined" (Verweij & Rao, 2017).

By understanding these benefits and implementing strategic measures as outlined in this chapter, you too can leverage technology for success. Now let's move toward action steps:

• Start with identifying areas where automation would prove beneficial.

• Seek expert advice if required.

• Choose a suitable software package or service provider after thorough research.

• Implement it gradually, checking progress regularly.

- Learn and upgrade continuously—necessary as technology evolves rapidly.

Remember: Success doesn't come overnight. Patience combined with hard work always prevails!

# CHAPTER 4:
# THE CONS TO OVERCOME

Artificial intelligence—AI—it's a term that swarms around modern businesses like bees to honey. Yet, just as those sweet-loving insects can sting, AI holds potential hazards for businesses.

This chapter will explore the dark underbelly of AI: ethical concerns, potential job losses due to automation, and data security risks. But don't fret! Equipped with knowledge and insight, we can navigate these landmines successfully.

Albert Einstein once said, "A person who never made a mistake never tried anything new." However, when it comes to AI in business, some mistakes could be costly. It's important to understand the possible pitfalls before diving headfirst into this brave new world.

## Chapter 4.1: Navigating the Ethical Concerns of AI in Business

In a bustling tech startup in Silicon Valley, an innovative project was underway. The team had designed an advanced artificial intelligence system to streamline their business operations. However, as the AI began making decisions that impacted employees and customers alike, ethical concerns started to surface.

The AI system, while efficient and capable of remarkable feats, seemed oblivious to certain aspects of fairness and transparency. For instance, it disproportionately recommended male candidates over females for promotion within the company based on historical data.

The team quickly recognized that while AI could potentially revolutionize their business operations, they would also need to navigate complex ethical waters. This realization marked their first step towards grappling with the ethics of implementing AI in business.

Just like this startup, every business seeking to leverage AI must understand these ethical considerations and develop strategies to address them effectively. This chapter will guide you through key ethical concerns related to using AI in your business and provide practical advice for overcoming them.

## Understanding Bias in Algorithms

Data is at the heart of any AI system. These systems learn from data patterns and make decisions based on those patterns. However, if the input data reflects societal biases or flawed processes, the resulting algorithm could unintentionally perpetuate these biases, leading to unfair outcomes.

To avoid this pitfall, ensure your datasets are balanced and reflect a fair representation of different demographics or variables relevant to your business context. Regularly audit your algorithms for bias and take corrective measures when necessary.

In her book *Atlas Of AI* (2021), Dr. Kate Crawford from Microsoft Research wrote, "Algorithms are not neutral; they are encoded with human biases." Understanding this will be pivotal in navigating the ethical challenges posed by biased algorithms.

Herein lies one of the major cons of using AI in business; navigating the ethical concerns is akin to walking through a minefield with a blindfold on.

## Transparency: An Essential Element

Transparency is another critical aspect when implementing AI in business contexts. Stakeholders need to understand how decisions made by an AI system were reached, particularly when these impact them directly.

Adopting explainable AI models can help address this issue— these models provide insights into how they reach conclusions or predictions. While more complex models may deliver higher accuracy rates, simplicity and transparency should never be compromised for performance alone.

Across the industry, experts and thought leaders have agreed that transparency builds trust in artificial intelligence. This underscores the importance of transparency when you begin integrating new technologies such as AI into your businesses.

## Balancing Progress With Ethics

While leveraging artificial intelligence can bring about significant advancements for your business operations, it's crucial not to lose sight of ethical considerations amidst technological pursuits.

By understanding these potential pitfalls associated with deploying artificial intelligence—such as biased decision-making processes or lack of transparency—you can proactively tackle these issues head-on.

Remember that treating ethics as an integral part of your technology strategy doesn't just prevent future crises. It also fosters trust among stakeholders— a priceless asset for any organization aiming at long-term success with artificial intelligence at its core.

# Chapter 4.2: Embracing Automation While Safeguarding Jobs

Natalie, a seasoned customer service representative for a leading telecom provider, felt a sense of unease creeping in as her company announced the integration of AI into their operations. The looming fear of job loss due to automation became a constant companion.

Contrary to Natalie's fears, however, the management had a well-planned transition system in place. Instead of replacing human agents with AI-powered bots outright, the company repositioned its employees into roles that capitalized on their unique human traits—empathy, creativity, and strategic thinking.

The AI system took over routine queries, freeing up time for human representatives to handle complex issues requiring emotional intelligence and critical problem-solving skills. Rather than losing her job, Natalie found herself excelling in an enhanced role with new challenges and opportunities for growth.

This segment of the chapter aims to address similar concerns about potential job losses due to automation and provide actionable strategies for companies looking to integrate AI without displacing their workforce.

## Understanding the Fear: Job Losses Due to Automation

Understandably, one of the most significant concerns surrounding AI adoption in businesses is potential job displacement. As machines become capable of performing tasks previously done by humans more efficiently and cost-effectively, it can trigger anxiety among employees.

Bill Gates once said: "The first rule of any technology used in a business is that automation applied to an efficient operation will magnify the efficiency" (Orr & Orr, 2014). However, it is crucial to remember that while automation enhances efficiency, it doesn't necessarily have to lead to mass unemployment.

Let's create another scenario—you've automated several processes within your company using AI solutions. Efficiency has skyrocketed, but at what cost? This newfound productivity has led to layoffs because manual jobs have become redundant.

While this may benefit bottom-line figures in the short term, consider an essential factor often overlooked when implementing automation strategies powered by artificial intelligence: long-term implications such as staff morale and public relations backlash from widespread job losses.

## Preparing Employees for the Future: Skill Upgradation and Reskilling

When integrating AI into your business operations, consider investing in reskilling initiatives for your employees. This can empower them with skills necessary not only to survive but thrive in an increasingly automated environment.

Training programs focusing on skills like leadership, creativity, or emotional intelligence—areas where humans still outperform machines—can help employees find new ways to add value.

Moreover, instilling confidence among employees through transparent communication about your intentions and plans regarding AI implementation can go a long way towards alleviating fears.

## Optimizing Human-AI Collaboration in Business

Rather than viewing AI as a replacement for human workers, consider it as an opportunity for collaboration where each party plays to its strengths. Machines excel at data processing and repetitive tasks while humans bring insightfulness and creative problem-solving abilities.

A survey conducted by Accenture revealed that 67% of workers believe AI will help them work more efficiently. When used correctly, AI can free up employee time spent on mundane tasks, allowing them more time focusing on challenging aspects that require human ingenuity.

## Balancing Efficiency With Empathy

We often fear what we do not understand—it's human nature. In terms of AI, this lack of understanding has led to unsettling tales of job losses and robot dominance. These stories echo through office corridors, feeding into people's natural resistance to change.

But let's consider a metaphor. Imagine if electricity were discovered today instead of over a century ago? We would have similar apprehensions about its use—dangers, possibility of misuse, or even potential job losses for candle makers! Yet today we can't fathom life without it.

Understanding is key to overcoming fears associated with AI implementation in business environments. When employees comprehend how AI can augment their roles rather than replace them, anxiety diminishes significantly.

While it's true that adopting artificial intelligence can streamline operations significantly and improve bottom-line results considerably, you mustn't do so at the cost of your most valuable asset—your people.

By understanding these concerns and implementing proactive strategies mentioned here, such as investing in reskilling initiatives, you'll not only be safeguarding jobs but also creating new opportunities within your organization.

It's crucial to always keep open lines of communication about how you plan on implementing these changes. Letting them know well beforehand what your plans are will likely reduce their stress levels around this change significantly.

As we've seen from Natalie's story outlined in this chapter, if done right, both parties (humans and robots) can actually work together harmoniously... And actually make everyone's lives easier!

## Chapter 4.3: Safeguarding Data and Privacy in AI Implementation

In the bustling city of San Francisco, a young entrepreneur named Lisa was on the verge of making her long-nurtured dream come true. She had worked tirelessly to develop an AI application that could automate customer service for businesses.

Her innovative creation was poised to revolutionize the industry. However, just before the launch, she faced a sudden setback. Her beta testers reported several occurrences of data breaches. Personal information entered into the AI system was accessible in raw form, putting user privacy at risk.

Lisa realized that while her focus had been on creating an efficient AI tool, she hadn't given enough attention to data security and privacy—elements crucial to any business operating in today's digital age.

Much like Lisa's situation, every business aspiring to leverage AI must be aware of and prepared for potential challenges related to data security and privacy. This part of the chapter will guide you through understanding these risks and provide practical advice on how to mitigate them.

## Understanding Data Security Risks With AI

Artificial intelligence thrives on data. It learns from it, grows with it, and becomes better because of it. However, this dependency on data also poses significant risks. As with Lisa's app, if not properly secured, customer information can become vulnerable.

"Data is the new oil," says mathematician Clive Humby, suggesting its immense value in today's digital economy (Janegar, n.d.). When so much depends on it, securing your data becomes paramount. Industry best practice is to implement robust measures such as encryption algorithms and multi-factor authentication systems for access control. Regular audits of your security protocols will ensure they remain effective against emerging threats.

## Respecting Privacy Laws While Leveraging AI

AI's capability to collect vast amounts of personal information raises concerns about user privacy. In response, numerous countries have implemented stringent laws regulating the collection and use of personal data by businesses. In America alone, there are over 20 sector-specific national privacy laws and hundreds more at the state level—each demanding compliance from businesses handling sensitive consumer information.

Thus, navigating these legal landscapes can be challenging but necessary for businesses using AI. Hiring a legal expert specializing in technology law or consulting legal resources online can help you stay compliant with these regulations.

As businesses increasingly rely on data-driven insights provided by AI systems, privacy concerns become paramount. It's essential to respect individual privacy rights while gathering data necessary for your algorithms.

Every organization must ensure its practices align with existing data protection laws like GDPR (General Data Protection Regulation) or CCPA (California Consumer Privacy Act), depending on geographical location and scope of operation.

Dr. Latanya Sweeney, who founded the Data Privacy Lab at Harvard University, warned about neglecting privacy considerations, stating (Perry, 2011):

One experiment after another has shown that people will make poor decisions about anything that involves their privacy. They want the new utility, they want the new shiny thing, because we tend to discount that any harm is going to happen to us, even when we're told that it could.

### *The Bottom Line: Minimizing Risk While Maximizing AI Potential*

While dealing with sensitive data and respecting privacy laws might seem daunting initially, remember that despite these challenges, implementing AI can greatly enhance your business operations when done responsibly.

The key lies in striking a balance between leveraging AI capabilities and minimizing associated risks through robust security measures and strict adherence to relevant laws.

Remember that safeguarding user data isn't merely about avoiding legal penalties; it also builds trust with customers who entrust their sensitive information to you. By being cognizant about potential security risks associated with using artificial intelligence—and taking proactive steps—you can not only ensure compliance but also gain consumer confidence.

In the same way as Lisa learned from her initial setback and eventually went on to successfully launch her app, you too can overcome security challenges by understanding how best to safeguard your users' interests while making full use of the benefits that artificial intelligence has to offer.

# CHAPTER 5:
# QUELLING THE STORM

*The world as we have created it is a process of our thinking. It cannot be changed without changing our thinking.*
—Albert Einstein

As businesses venture into the uncharted waters of artificial intelligence, this quote by Albert Einstein takes on a new significance. The fear and skepticism that surround AI in the business arena are like dark clouds looming over an otherwise sunny horizon. This chapter will shed light on these murky areas, guiding you through the storm.

## Chapter 5.1: Overcoming Fear and Skepticism Around AI

In a bustling tech startup, Gary, an experienced data analyst, was known for his meticulous attention to detail and quick problem-solving skills. However, when the company decided to integrate artificial intelligence into their operations, Gary found himself grappling with uncertainty.

At first, he saw AI as a threat, fearing it might render his role obsolete. He also questioned if an algorithm could match human intuition and experience. Despite his reservations, Gary decided to confront these fears head-on and began learning about AI.

With time and effort, he discovered that AI was not his replacement but rather a tool designed to enhance human capacity. It took over repetitive tasks, freeing up his time for more complex problem-solving. His new understanding transformed his skepticism into enthusiasm. Gary's journey is emblematic of the apprehension many face in embracing AI in business.

This chapter aims to address your concerns around incorporating AI into your business operations and provide practical advice on how you can shift from skepticism to acceptance.

## Unveiling AI, and Settling Fear of It

The fear of the unknown is often the root cause of resistance towards technological advancements like AI. It's crucial to educate yourself and your team about what exactly AI is and how it can be beneficial rather than detrimental.

According to Andrew Ng, co-founder of Google Brain, "AI is akin to electricity—it radically transformed industries across the board when it was introduced" (Lynch, 2017).

Integrating AI into your business isn't about replacing humans. Rather, it's about automating mundane tasks while increasing productivity and efficiency.

## Addressing Job Security Concerns

One of the biggest fears employees have regarding introducing AI into their workplace revolves around job security—will they be replaced by machines?

A report by McKinsey Global Institute (*A future that works...*, 2017) states the following:

While less than 5 percent of all occupations can be automated entirely using demonstrated technologies, about 60% of all occupations have at least 30% of constituent activities that could be automated.

The report goes on to suggest that, rather than eliminating jobs outright, AI will transform them or create new ones. This shift may require upskilling or reskilling, but it certainly doesn't signal mass unemployment.

## Debunking Myths: Can Machines Outsmart Humans?

Another common skepticism stems from doubts whether machines can ever truly match or surpass human intelligence.

While it's true that machines are capable of processing vast amounts of data remarkably faster than humans and identifying patterns through machine learning algorithms, at present they lack creativity, social awareness, and emotional intelligence—inherently human qualities.

Dr. Fei-Fei Li, a renowned computer science professor at Stanford University, states that "humanity is defined by its collective intelligence—our culture, knowledge, institutions. We need to bring this collective-intelligence spirit to nurture artificial intelligence" (Stanford Online, 2023).

## *The Bottom Line: Embracing Change and Achieving Potential*

*Change is hard at first, messy in the middle, and gorgeous*
*at the end.*
–Robin Sharma

It's normal for change to incite fear. However, hiding behind skepticism won't prevent progress. It's high time we start viewing artificial intelligence as an ally rather than an adversary.

By dispelling myths, facing fears, and proactively engaging in continuous learning, you'll discover that integrating artificial intelligence within your business operations can revolutionize productivity, optimize efficiency, and open doors for innovation—just like it did for Gary.

# Chapter 5.2: Embracing AI: Preparing Employees for an AI-Driven Workplace

Susan, a long-time accounting manager at a mid-sized manufacturing firm, had heard the rumblings about AI coming to change the workplace. She watched as her company started implementing new systems and heard management talk about "efficiency" and "automation." Susan was worried. As someone who wasn't particularly tech-savvy, she feared being left behind or, worse yet, replaced by machines.

It wasn't until her company held an AI workshop that Susan's fears began to abate. The workshop helped her understand AI and illustrated how it could assist rather than replace human employees. Susan then realized that this technological transition was not a threat but an opportunity—an opportunity to learn new skills and improve efficiency in her work.

Much like Susan, many employees may feel anxious or skeptical about the integration of AI into their workplaces. This chapter aims to provide guidance on addressing these fears and preparing your workforce for a smooth transition into an AI-driven environment.

## Understanding AI's Role in the Workplace

Artificial intelligence is not here to eliminate jobs but to augment humans' capabilities. It can do this by automating mundane tasks, thus freeing up time for more strategic and creative work—a truly transformative feat. It's essential to communicate this clearly with your team; emphasize that AI is a tool designed to enhance their abilities rather than replace them.

## Training Sessions and Workshops

Holding training sessions and workshops can allay fears and clear misconceptions about AI much like it did for Susan. Hands-on exposure allows employees to understand how they can use these technologies in their daily tasks, making them feel more comfortable with the transition.

## Bridging Knowledge Gaps

Not everyone in your organization will have the same level of familiarity with technology. To ensure everyone benefits from the implementation of AI equally, offer skill-upgrade opportunities—whether through online courses or training programs—to those who need it most.

## Empowering Participation

A study by McKinsey (Dhingra et al., 2021) suggests that employees who believe their jobs have meaning, or that they are part of significant change efforts, are more adaptable:

"People who live their purpose at work are more productive than people who don't. They are also healthier, more resilient, and more likely to stay at the company...the benefits expand to include stronger employee engagement, heightened loyalty, and a greater willingness to recommend the company to others."

So encourage your employees to take part in decision-making processes related to AI implementation. When they feel involved and heard, they're more likely to embrace changes positively.

## Ensuring Job Security

Reassure your staff that while roles may change slightly due to automation, their positions within the company remain secure. Highlight instances where automation has led to job growth within industries—like how ATMs resulted in more bank tellers— as proof of concept.

# Chapter 5.3: Navigating the Waves of Change

Under the bustling streets of London, Tom Collins, a tube operator for over two decades, faced an impending change that threatened his livelihood. The London Underground was planning to implement automated train operation (ATO), replacing human operators with artificial intelligence.

Tom, like many other employees, was skeptical and fearful of this transition. However, the management team at London Underground realized they had to address these fears and embarked on a plan to help their team understand and embrace AI.

They started by involving Tom in training programs designed to show how AI could improve efficiency while still requiring human intervention for decision-making processes. By being included in this transition process, Tom began to appreciate the benefits of AI and see how his role would adapt rather than disappear.

Like the London Underground example, many businesses today face resistance when introducing AI into their operations. This chapter will guide you through understanding these fears and offer strategies for managing change effectively.

## Understanding Employee Fears Around AI

Fear of job loss is one of the most significant concerns employees have when it comes to implementing AI in business processes.

While it's true that automation may replace certain tasks, it also creates new roles that didn't exist before.

Incorporating your team into the transition process can help alleviate these fears. Training programs can demonstrate how employees' roles might evolve with AI integration, rather than be eliminated by it.

Remember that study by McKinsey & Company which said that about 60% of all occupations have at least 30% technically-automatable activities? However, this doesn't necessarily mean job losses, but instead signifies a shift in what those jobs will entail.

## Managing Resistance to Change

Just as every individual has unique talents and skills, each person also has their own comfort level with change. Some may welcome innovation while others resist it out of fear or uncertainty. It's essential, then, to manage this resistance by communicating openly about changes and providing ample support during transitions.

As we stand on the precipice of a new era, where AI stands ready to revolutionize how we do business, it's vital that we understand change is not only inevitable but necessary. The transition from traditional manual jobs to AI-backed automated roles might seem daunting. However, it can be navigated smoothly with a comprehensive change management strategy.

Let's delve into this further by examining some key elements of successful change management strategies for transitioning to AI.

1. **Acknowledge the Change:** The first step towards managing change effectively is acceptance. Imagine if our ancestors had shied away from discovering fire because they found it scary?

Similarly, fearing AI isn't going to aid progress; accepting its potential is!

2. **Educate Stakeholders:** Knowledge dispels fear! When stakeholders understand what AI can do—its benefits, limitations, and implications for their roles—they're less likely to resist the transformation process.

3. **Train and Equip Employees:** Another critical component in transitioning towards using AI in business is addressing the skills gap among current employees. Upskilling them ensures they're not lost as automation takes over certain tasks but are instead equipped to manage these new systems efficiently. Offering training programs not only enables staff members to understand how AI works but also equips them with abilities needed for its effective implementation.

A report by PwC found that 77% of CEOs view a lack of skills as the greatest threat to their business (*20th CEO Survey*, 2017). Addressing this issue head-on can promote employee confidence and smooth transitions towards embracing new technology within your company's operations.

4. **Provide Ongoing Support:** Remember that even seasoned sailors sometimes struggle with high tides! Offering continuous support post-transition helps allay fears and address challenges promptly.

5. **Celebrate Milestones:** Small victories lead to big successes! Celebrating milestones keeps morale high during this crucial phase of transition.

For a more detailed change strategy, look into Kotter's 8-Step Change Model, which includes creating urgency around the need for change; forming a powerful coalition; forming strategic visions; enlisting volunteers; removing obstacles; generating short-term wins; sustaining acceleration; and instituting change.

Now let's consider what happens when businesses don't manage changes properly, using an analogy familiar to everyone—weeds growing out of control in your garden! Unmanaged transitions are like allowing weeds free reign; they choke out healthy growth, ultimately leading to decay instead of flourishing ecosystems (or businesses).

So how does one ensure their "business garden" thrives amid this significant shift?

Firstly, don't ignore those "weeds" (resistance)! Addressing concerns promptly prevents minor issues from escalating into major roadblocks later on—like pulling out weeds before they overrun your garden!

Secondly, nourish your "plants" (employees). Regular training sessions keep them updated about the latest trends so they can adapt quickly—much like timely watering enables plants grow stronger, faster!

Lastly, remember that just as gardens require regular maintenance for optimal health, so too do organizations undergoing transitions!

In conclusion,

- Acceptance is paramount.

- Education dispels resistance.

- Training equips employees for future challenges.

- Continuous support aids smooth transitions.

- Celebration fuels motivation during challenging times.

These points form our roadmap, guiding us through the turbulent waters of transitioning towards an AI-driven business environment successfully while ensuring minimal upheaval within organization structure and workflows alike!

Remember Einstein's words: "The measure of intelligence is the ability to adapt to change." As we embrace artificial intelligence and adapt the way we conduct business, let us also strive to become intelligent, adaptable entities ourselves by navigating the journey ahead more confidently and sure-footedly, despite uncertainties lurking around the corner!

## An Example of Successful Change

The first time I met Peter, he was the CEO of a successful manufacturing company. His company had built its reputation on quality and precision, which largely depended on skilled workers who meticulously crafted each part by hand. The operation ran as smoothly as a well-oiled machine, but there was one small problem: It wasn't scalable.

Peter knew that in order to grow his business and remain competitive, he needed to automate certain tasks using artificial intelligence. However, he also understood that this would potentially mean laying off some of his employees—people who had been with him since day one. This weighed heavily on Peter's conscience.

He asked himself an important question: "How can I transition my business into the new era of AI without causing unnecessary harm to my loyal staff?"

This is a common dilemma faced by leaders across industries today. The advent of AI presents tremendous opportunities for businesses but also comes with challenges related to change management.

In search of answers, Peter started researching different strategies for managing change during technological transitions. He looked into various options, from training current employees in handling new technology to evaluating potential roles where human intervention would still be crucial even after automation.

One day, while discussing his predicament with a fellow CEO at an industry conference, she suggested something unexpected: "Make your employees feel involved in the transition."

Peter thought about this advice deeply. What if instead of fearing their replacement by machines, his staff felt like they were actively participating in shaping the future direction of the company? Could this shift in perspective make all the difference?

With renewed determination, Peter returned home and immediately set up a meeting with all his employees, explaining his vision for integrating AI into their operations. He listened attentively to their concerns and suggestions and assured them that no decision would be made without considering their input.

To facilitate this process further, Peter introduced regular workshops aimed at educating everyone about artificial intelligence—what it meant for their industry and how it could potentially impact their jobs. These sessions were not just informative; they allowed everyone within the organization to voice out questions or worries while fostering a sense of camaraderie among staff members facing similar uncertainties together.

As weeks turned into months, something remarkable happened: Employees began sharing innovative ideas about how AI could be incorporated into their work processes effectively without completely replacing manual labor. They saw ways around problems that weren't previously visible when viewed from top-level management's perspective alone.

Through this inclusive approach towards change management during the AI adoption phase, not only did Peter manage to successfully automate parts of production without any significant layoffs, but he also fostered an environment where every individual felt valued as an integral part of the overall growth story—despite the looming threat posed by technological advancements such as artificial intelligence.

And so we see that implementing comprehensive change management strategies can indeed help businesses navigate this tricky transitional phase competently while leaving no employee behind.

## The Bottom Line: Facing Change Together

If you find yourself standing where Peter once stood, looking at the daunting task ahead as you contemplate switching over to automated counterparts backed by AI, remember that introducing artificial intelligence into your business operations doesn't have to be daunting at all—if handled correctly. Much like Susan's experience shows us, it's all about understanding AI's role better, and involving everyone onboard during this transformational journey.

By addressing fear of change and fostering understanding early on, you can prepare your workforce for an efficient and harmonious transition towards an exciting future powered by artificial intelligence.

*Key takeaway: Change is inevitable, especially when it comes to tech-reliant industries. However, its impact can be managed proactively through effective communication, transparency, and education, in conjunction with re-skilling initiatives which ensure a smooth transition period with minimal collateral damage.*

# CHAPTER 6:
# HUMANIZING YOUR BRAND IN
# AN AGE OF AUTOMATION

In the bustling heart of Silicon Valley, a tech startup was unlocking new horizons with their AI-driven customer service system. As their client base grew, they leveraged automation to manage queries and complaints more efficiently. But soon, customers started expressing dissatisfaction with the impersonal interactions.

The founders took note and decided to tweak their approach. They trained their AI bots to show empathy, use conversational language, and even sprinkle in a bit of humor at appropriate times. The results? A surge in customer satisfaction and loyalty. This experience highlighted the significance of balancing automation with a personal touch in today's business world.

How does a brand strike a balance between leveraging automation technology for operational efficiency while still retaining its human side? One way is through designing a customer-centric chatbot experience. This involves programming your chatbot not just to respond mechanically based on pre-set scripts but also to learn from each interaction and refine its responses over time.

Furthermore, integrating voice-enabled assistants within your product/service offerings can add another layer of personalization. For instance, instead of typing out their queries or commands on their smartphones or computers, customers can simply talk to these virtual assistants as if they were talking to another person. Simulating that sort of interpersonal interaction which lies at the heart of every successful brand-customer relationship is key.

There's ample evidence supporting this claim, too. In a report by Capgemini Research Institute titled *The Secret To Winning Customers' Hearts With Artificial Intelligence: Add Human Intelligence* (Buvat et al., 2018), they found that companies blending AI with human collaboration saw significantly higher growth rates compared to those using AI alone.

Take for example Starbucks's mobile app, which uses predictive analytics combined with baristas' expertise in recommending personalized drink options based on customers' previous orders. Another example is Sephora's Virtual Artist app, which combines augmented reality (AR) with expert advice, allowing users to try different makeup products virtually before making actual purchases.

*The most productive thing you will have done in your life is empowering people... Technology is just a tool.*
–Satya Nadella

Automating processes has clear benefits, such as cost reduction and enhanced productivity, but when it comes down to forming deep connections with customers, emotions play a pivotal role which machines cannot entirely replicate yet.

## Chapter 6.1: Understanding Your Customers' Needs

At the core of every successful business is an understanding of its customers' needs. Automation can help cater to these needs swiftly, but may lack the personal touch humans inherently crave.

Author and business expert Shep Hyken notes that "the greatest technology in the world hasn't replaced the ultimate relationship-building tool between a customer and a business—the human touch" (Quiseng, n.d.).

Harnessing AI capabilities while preserving this human aspect could be your key to winning clients over.

## Balancing Efficiency With Empathy

Automation has drastically improved efficiency levels across various sectors. Still, businesses must remember that it's not just about delivering quick solutions; it's also about showing empathy towards your customers' concerns.

A study by Harvard Business Review found that "emotionally engaged customers are three times more likely to recommend a product or service" (McGilvrey, n.d.).

Train your AI systems to pick up on emotional cues from customers and respond accordingly. This balance between speed and empathy can substantially enhance your customers' experience.

## Creating Authentic Interactions

To effectively humanize your brand, create authentic interactions for your customers. Incorporate personalized messaging into automated emails or chatbots based on users' behavior or preferences.

For instance, Spotify uses AI algorithms to curate personalized playlists for each user—a perfect example of using automation while maintaining individuality.

A report by Epsilon (2018) revealed that:

- "80% of consumers are more likely to make a purchase when brands offer personalized experiences."

- Over two-thirds of consumers globally prefer speaking to live agents over interacting with automated systems for resolving complaints and complex issues.

- Companies successfully combining AI and human services witness an up-to-60% increase in revenue generation compared to peers relying solely on one or the other.

- About half of the global consumers are willing to share more data if the brands promise to enhance shopping experiences with tailored suggestions and helpful tips.

These findings stress how vital it is for companies to provide unique experiences for each customer despite using automated systems.

**Example 1:**

I once had the privilege to visit a real estate firm that had recently incorporated AI in their customer service department. They had developed an intelligent chatbot, named "Bella," who was designed to answer basic queries of potential clients and only transfer complex queries to human agents.

When I spoke with the CEO, he shared how Bella transformed their customer service operations. "Our call wait times have reduced by half," he said, displaying an impressive graph on his tablet. But what intrigued me most wasn't the efficiency brought about by Bella; it was her ability to connect with customers on a personal level.

The CEO told me about an incident where a lady reached out through their website's live chat at 2:00 A.M. She wanted information about a property but seemed unsure and hesitant while asking questions. Instead of just providing cut-and-dry answers, Bella sensed the hesitation in the customer's tone and responded empathetically—asking if she needed more time or additional resources to make her decision. The lady was so touched by this thoughtful interaction that she sent the company an appreciative email later.

This story stayed with me for days because it made one thing clear: In today's age of automation, we must not forget the importance of human touch.

As companies increasingly leverage AI for improving efficiency and productivity, there's often a concern that we might end up losing our brand's human touch—the essence that separates us from machines. However, as demonstrated by Bella, when implemented correctly, artificial intelligence can help us amplify our empathy rather than suppress it.

**Example 2:**

A popular online clothing retailer decided to integrate voice-enabled assistants within their product offerings. Their AI assistant helps users find clothes based on preferences expressed in natural language—like color preference or style choice—and even offers personalized suggestions based on past purchases.

This has significantly enhanced user experience, as browsing through hundreds of items became much simpler and more enjoyable—an excellent example of how conversational AIs can enhance customer engagement levels without sacrificing personalization.

Of course, integrating such technology involves cost. But when you factor in increased customer satisfaction and repeat business—which are likely outcomes if you implement these technologies thoughtfully—the ROI becomes quite compelling indeed.

But here is the caveat: While incorporating AI within your business model can bring numerous benefits, like reducing workload for employees or providing round-the-clock assistance, it should never be viewed as a replacement for humans but rather as a supplement that enhances your team's capabilities further.

Remember, you're not trying to create robots devoid of emotion; instead, aim for creating intelligent systems capable of understanding emotions better. Just like how Bella turned that hesitant lady into a satisfied client with an empathetic response, it's all about finding ways to provide value while maintaining warmth and empathy—that's how you "humanize" your brand despite living amidst increasing automation!

By striking this balance between automation and personal touch, companies could reap substantial benefits both regarding efficiency improvements and as enhanced customer satisfaction levels! So, next time you think about automating any part of your business, remember—it's not just about reducing costs or increasing speed. It's also very much about fostering meaningful connections with customers, even in this age dominated by artificial intelligence.

## Chapter 6.2: Designing a Customer-Centric Chatbot Experience

In the bustling city of New York, a small start-up called Nifty thrived amidst fierce competition. Their secret weapon? A chatbot named "NiftyBot." This friendly AI interface was their primary customer service representative, handling everything from product inquiries to issue resolution.

When customers interacted with NiftyBot, they weren't met with robotic responses. Instead, they experienced a warm conversation that felt human-like. NiftyBot was programmed to understand complex questions, respond empathetically, and even use humor when appropriate.

The result? An increase in customer satisfaction and loyalty for the brand. Nifty's success story is a testament to the power of well-designed chatbots in providing excellent customer service while enhancing brand image.

This section will guide you on how to create a similar experience for your business by designing an effective, customer-centric chatbot that not only handles queries but also adds a personal touch to every interaction it has with your customers.

## Creating an Engaging Chatbot Experience

A chatbot can be as simple or as sophisticated as you make it. The key lies in creating an engaging experience. It's about striking a balance between utility and personality.

For instance, Domino's Pizza introduced "Dom," its pizza-ordering bot who not only takes orders but also engages customers with his quirky character. This clever approach has made ordering pizza more fun and engaging for customers all over the world.

According to Grand View Research, "the global chatbot market size is expected to reach USD 1.25 billion by 2025," which underscores the importance of integrating this technology into your business operations (Sundstrom, 2023).

## Designing for Customer Needs

Beyond personality, your chatbot should be designed to meet specific customer needs efficiently. Whether it's answering queries about products or services or resolving complaints promptly, ensure your bot is equipped with relevant information and can provide solutions quickly.

Take Sephora's Kik bot for example; it offers personalized beauty advice based on individual preferences and needs. By integrating data analysis into bot programming, Sephora managed to create a highly responsive tool that enhances the overall shopping experience.

## Emphasizing Natural Language Processing

While functionality is crucial in designing your bot, don't overlook the importance of natural language processing. NLP allows bots like NiftyBot or Dom to understand context and nuances during conversations with customers and react accordingly.

Let's take another example: A popular online clothing retailer decided to integrate voice-enabled assistants within their product offerings. Their AI assistant helps users find clothes based on preferences expressed in natural language—like color preference or style choice—and even offers personalized suggestions based on past purchases. This has significantly enhanced user experience, as it made browsing through hundreds of items much simpler and more enjoyable—an excellent example of how conversational AIs can enhance customer engagement levels without sacrificing personalization.

Bots utilizing advanced NLP can interpret complicated requests accurately and offer precise solutions without requiring human intervention—an efficiency that greatly improves user experience.

## Making Your Bot More Human-Like

Ultimately, creating an effective AI-driven customer service strategy means developing a chatbot that embodies your brand while meeting consumer needs efficiently—just like Nifty did with their affable NiftyBot.

By focusing on engagement strategies alongside technical capabilities such as data integration and natural language processing, you can successfully humanize your brand through automation.

## The Bottom Line: Balancing Automation With Personal Touch

In an age where businesses are increasingly relying on automation and artificial intelligence, never underestimate the power of adding a personal touch. Remember: you're catering not just to users or accounts, but to individuals who appreciate authenticity and empathy.

As you take these steps towards implementing AI into your business operations, remember that, at heart, it's about preserving the human touch amidst technological advancements and creating intelligent systems capable of understanding emotions better!

By blending efficient automated systems with elements that humanize your brand—understanding customer needs, showing empathy, creating authentic interactions—you ensure longevity in an era dominated by technology without losing sight of what makes us fundamentally human.

*Key Takeaway: Automation shouldn't replace humans; rather, it should augment our capabilities. It's about finding the right blend between digital innovation and the human touch.*

# CHAPTER 7:
# EXPLORING APPLICATION AREAS FOR AI IN DIFFERENT INDUSTRIES

Artificial intelligence isn't just about robots taking over the world; it's about making businesses smarter and more efficient. Evidence of its influence is undeniable across industries. According to Accenture research, AI could double annual economic growth rates by 2035 by changing the nature of work and creating new relationships between man and machine.

Let us explore how different sectors are leveraging artificial intelligence.

## Chapter 7.1: The Role of AI in Medical Imaging

Healthcare has been one of the early adopters of AI, with groundbreaking applications like robot-assisted surgeries which provide precision beyond human capabilities; predictive analytics tools that forecast patient deterioration based on real-time data; intelligent prosthetics with sensors that adjust motion using machine learning algorithms; and drug discovery platforms employing deep learning techniques for rapid screening of molecules.

In the bustling city of Boston, Massachusetts General Hospital was facing a significant challenge. The radiology department was overwhelmed with the volume of imaging data they had to process and interpret every day. With an increasing number of patients relying on their services, the radiologists found it increasingly difficult to keep up with the work pace.

Then came an unexpected solution—artificial intelligence. The hospital began implementing AI algorithms designed to analyze and interpret medical images. These AI systems worked alongside human experts, significantly reducing their workload and improving diagnosis accuracy.

This transformation at Massachusetts General Hospital is only one example of how healthcare has flourished thanks to AI. This chapter will delve into understanding these applications and offer insights into how you can leverage AI in healthcare.

Medical imaging is a critical component in diagnosing various diseases. However, interpreting these images requires considerable expertise and time. Here's where AI steps in.

AI algorithms can be trained to recognize patterns in medical images such as X-rays, MRIs, or CT scans. Once trained, these algorithms can identify abnormalities that might indicate potential health issues faster than human radiologists while reducing errors.

A study by Stanford University discovered that "an algorithm outperformed radiologists when differentiating between malignant and benign lesions on ultrasound images" (Kubota, 2017).

AI not only assists doctors but also has the potential to revolutionize patient care by speeding up diagnosis times.

### Predictive Analytics: A Proactive Approach

Another exciting application area for AI in healthcare is predictive analytics—using historical data to predict future outcomes or trends. Meet Dr. Sarah, a renowned surgeon who has been integrating AI into her daily work. She told me about how she used predictive analytics to forecast future events. It helped her identify high-risk patients early on so she could focus more on preventive care, improving patient outcomes while reducing costs for the hospital.

By analyzing past patient records, symptoms, or genetic information, AI systems can predict disease risk factors or anticipate potential health issues before they become severe problems. This proactive approach could potentially save lives while easing the strain on healthcare providers.

According to research from McKinsey & Company (Cattell, et al., 2013): "Applying predictive analytics in healthcare could save up to $100 billion annually in the US healthcare system by improving efficiency and quality."

## Personalized Medicine: Tailoring Treatment Plans

AI holds remarkable promise for personalized medicine—tailoring treatment plans based on a patient's unique genetic makeup or health history. By analyzing a person's genome sequencing data using machine learning techniques, physicians can customize treatments that are more effective for individual patients, thereby improving overall care quality.

As agreed by one cross-institutional team of scientists (Johnson et al., 2020): "The convergence of artificial intelligence (AI) and precision medicine promises to revolutionize health care."

## *The Bottom Line: Using AI Technology for Better Health Outcomes*

Without a doubt, embracing technology like artificial intelligence is essential for better health outcomes in today's fast-paced world.

Whether it's aiding doctors with medical imaging interpretation, predicting potential health risks through analytics, or personalizing treatment plans, leveraging AI presents immense opportunities for enhancing patient care quality while making significant cost savings.

Just like Massachusetts General Hospital turned around its radiology department with the help of AI, understanding its applications discussed here will enable you to harness this powerful technology effectively within your own healthcare-sector organization.

## Chapter 7.2: The Benefits of AI in Retail

At first glance, Taylor's business—a trendy boutique nestled in the heart of downtown—seemed like any other fashion store. Filled with vibrant clothes and accessories, it attracted both locals and tourists. However, behind the scenes, Taylor was revolutionizing her retail operations by integrating artificial intelligence.

With AI-powered tools, she was able to analyze customer behavior, personalize their shopping experience, automate inventory management, and even predict future trends. The result? Improved efficiency, increased sales, and enhanced customer satisfaction.

Taylor's story illustrates how AI is transforming an age-old industry like retail into a technology-driven one. This segment of the chapter will guide you through understanding the practical applications of AI in retail and offer insights on how to leverage this technology for your business.

### AI-Powered Personalization: A Game-Changer

Personalization is no longer a luxury but an expectation among consumers. In fact, Accenture (2018) found that "91% of consumers are more likely to shop with brands who provide offers and recommendations that are relevant to them."

AI can analyze vast amounts of data about customers' preferences and shopping habits to offer personalized recommendations. These could be product suggestions based on their past purchases or targeted promotions tailored to their needs.

By harnessing AI's power for personalization like Taylor did, businesses can boost customer engagement while maximizing revenue from each interaction.

## Inventory Management: From Guesswork to Precision

Managing inventory is a complex task that requires accurate prediction of demand to avoid stockouts or overstock situations. With AI's predictive analytics capabilities, retailers can forecast demand more accurately by considering factors such as historical sales data, seasonality trends, and market dynamics. Such precision leads to optimized inventory levels, which translate into cost savings due to reduced storage expenses and minimized losses from unsold items.

Managing inventory manually is time-consuming and prone to error. An AI-powered inventory management system tracks stock levels accurately in real time and can automatically reorder supplies when they run low.

A report from McKinsey Global Institute (*A future that works…*, 2017) stated that "Automation could raise productivity growth globally by 0.8–1.4 percent annually."

Enhancing productivity through automation allows you more time for strategic decision-making while reducing costs related to manual errors or oversupply issues.

### AI-Driven Trend Forecasting: Staying Ahead of the Curve

In the fast-paced world of retail where trends change rapidly, staying ahead of the curve is paramount. Traditional methods involve relying on intuition or previous seasons' sales records, which often leads to errors.

With AI's machine learning algorithms analyzing vast amounts of data across different channels—social media chatter, online reviews or search engine queries—retailers can identify emerging trends faster than ever before. This proactive approach allows businesses like Taylor's boutique to stay competitive by offering products aligned with what customers want at any given time.

### *The Bottom Line: Joining the AI Revolution*

For any retail business owner looking towards growth and innovation in this digital era—whether you're running a small boutique like Taylor or heading a large department store—embracing the power of AI isn't just beneficial; it's essential. By understanding its potential applications—from personalization strategies through inventory management all the way to up-to-the-minute trend forecasting—you'll be well-equipped to navigate this exciting new frontier in the retail industry.

Start exploring today how these technologies might fit within your current operations because, as we have seen from Taylor's experience, when harnessed correctly, they deliver fantastic results.

### Chapter 7.3: Harnessing the Power of AI in Marketing

Every morning, Molly, a marketing manager at a mid-sized retail company, sifted through piles of customer data. She spent hours analyzing buying patterns and behaviors, trying to map out strategies that would attract more customers. Despite her best efforts, Molly often felt overwhelmed by the sheer volume of information and was uncertain if her approaches were truly effective.

Then she discovered artificial intelligence. With AI's power, she could quickly analyze large sets of data and derive actionable insights. It helped her predict customer behavior with remarkable accuracy, enabling her to tailor marketing campaigns to resonate with specific audiences. The results were impressive: higher engagement rates, increased conversions, and improved customer satisfaction.

Just like Molly, you too can harness the power of AI for your marketing needs. This chapter will guide you on how to effectively use AI to transform your marketing strategies and achieve better results.

## Decoding Customer Behavior With AI

Deciphering customer behavior is crucial for any successful marketing strategy. By leveraging AI-powered predictive analytics tools, you can gain deep insights into consumer purchasing habits and preferences.

AI does this by analyzing historical data points and identifying patterns that inform future buying behavior predictions. This allows you to anticipate what your customers want even before they know it themselves.

According to a study by Boston Consulting Group (BCG, n.d.), "brands that create personalized experiences by integrating advanced digital technologies are seeing revenue increase by 6% to 10%."

By understanding your customers on this deeper level, you can curate personalized experiences that align with their expectations and enhance their overall experience with your brand.

## Improve Customer Service Through Chatbots

AI-powered chatbots have revolutionized customer service in many industries. These automated programs simulate human conversation and provide instant responses to customer queries round-the-clock. They not only improve efficiency but also offer immediate support, enhancing the overall customer experience.

Introducing an AI chatbot into your marketing mix ensures you're staying ahead of the curve in providing seamless customer service while freeing up time for other strategic tasks.

## Optimizing Content Creation

In our digitally-driven world, content is king; however, creating engaging content consistently can be challenging for marketers. Thanks to advancements in natural language processing, an aspect of AI technology now has the ability to generate human-like text based on data input.

These tools can help produce compelling product descriptions or blog posts, saving valuable time without compromising quality or creativity.

## Transforming Social Media Engagement

Social media platforms are treasure troves of consumer data waiting to be analyzed intelligently for marketing gains. With AI tools such as sentiment analysis algorithms or image recognition software at your disposal, you can understand how consumers feel about your brand or products based on their online interactions.

This real-time feedback allows marketers like yourself to respond promptly and address any issues raised, thereby improving brand perception among consumers.

One marketing director shared with me how his team used natural language processing to analyze thousands of social media posts within minutes to gauge public sentiment around their brand—something which would have taken weeks if done manually.

### *The Bottom Line: Empowering Enhanced Marketing Results With AI*

As we've established, embracing AI technology in your business strategy is no longer an option but a necessity if you wish to stay competitive in today's fast-paced digital landscape.

Remember, it's not about replacing humans, but rather augmenting their abilities by empowering them with intelligent insights which help make informed decisions quickly.

By incorporating the practical advice outlined in this chapter, you'll be well-equipped to not just survive but thrive in the era of artificial intelligence.

## Chapter 7.4: Harnessing the Power of AI in Manufacturing and Shipping

Imagine a bustling manufacturing facility owned by a company named MetaMachines. The assembly lines are buzzing with precision, products are being churned out at an impressive speed, and shipments are going out on time, every time. All this while the plant operates with lean staff, minimizes waste, and optimizes energy usage. The secret behind their success? The implementation of AI technologies.

When MetaMachines first ventured into AI integration, they faced resistance from their workforce due to fears of job displacement. But instead of replacing human workers, AI enhanced their roles. It took over repetitive tasks while employees shifted towards more strategic duties like supervision, quality control, and decision-making.

Like MetaMachines, you can also leverage AI to transform your manufacturing processes and shipping operations. This area of the chapter will guide you through understanding the potential application areas for AI in different industries and offer practical advice on how to harness its power effectively.

## Integrating AI in Production Processes

The use of artificial intelligence in production processes has been revolutionary. For large-scale manufacturers especially, it is mission-critical.

AI-powered robots can perform tasks with precision that surpasses human capability. They can work tirelessly without breaks or sleep, increasing output significantly. Moreover, predictive maintenance powered by machine learning can help prevent breakdowns before they happen by analyzing patterns in machinery behavior over time.

At a car manufacturing plant outside Detroit where robots have long replaced humans on assembly lines, these machines are now being equipped with image recognition capabilities, allowing them not only assemble parts but also inspect them for defects far quicker and more accurately than any human ever could.

A report published by McKinsey Global Institute (Bughin et al., 2018) states that "AI technologies could lead to an additional global economic activity of around $13 trillion by 2030." This emphasizes the enormous potential that lies within AI for businesses willing to adopt it.

## Optimizing Shipping Operations With AI

Shipping operations stand to gain immensely from AI integration as well. Intelligent algorithms can streamline logistics planning by optimizing routes based on real-time traffic data and weather forecasts.

AI can also automate warehousing operations such as inventory management and order picking—significantly reducing error rates and improving efficiency.

BCG's study also suggests that "companies that fully absorb digital technology into their supply chains can boost annual growth earnings before interest and taxes by 3.2 percent—the largest increase from digitizing any business area—and annual revenue growth by 2.3 percent."

### Utilizing Space Effectively Through Smart Layouts

Your manufacturing facility needs effective utilization of space for optimal performance—something achievable through smart layouts enabled by AI.

Artificial intelligence can analyze multiple variables like machine dimensions, material flow paths, worker safety zones, etc., to design efficient factory layouts, minimizing wasted movement and enhancing productivity levels.

## The Bottom Line: Powering Efficient Operations With AI

To unlock the full potential of your manufacturing business in this age of rapid technological advancement, you need not fear innovation, but instead embrace it wholeheartedly!

By integrating artificial intelligence into your production processes and shipping operations, you too can achieve operational excellence marked with higher productivity levels, lower error rates, and reduced waste—all leading towards increased profitability!

This journey begins with understanding the value addition brought about by these technologies, followed by strategic planning and implementation—something this chapter has aimed at facilitating for you.

As I reflected back on what I'd learned over these visits across different industries—healthcare, retail, marketing, and manufacturing—it became evident that artificial intelligence is no longer just hype; it's impacting business operations at every level, across sectors. And those willing to embrace this wave are reaping significant benefits: improved efficiency, reduced costs, higher-quality products/services, happier customers... The list goes on!

So whether you're a doctor, retailer, marketer, or manufacturer, don't wait to start exploring opportunities to integrate artificial intelligence into your business today and see magic happen.

**Key Takeaways:**

1. Artificial intelligence has broad applications across various industries including healthcare, retail, marketing, and manufacturing.

2. Predictive analytics, machine learning, natural language processing, and image recognition are some forms of AI technologies being leveraged.

3. Integrating AI can lead to improved efficiency, cost reduction, higher-quality products/services, and enhanced customer experience, among other benefits.

4. Leveraging AI is not about replacing humans, but rather about augmenting our abilities and allowing us to do much more, better and faster!

# CHAPTER 8:
# ADVANCED TOPICS IN ARTIFICIAL INTELLIGENCE

Understanding the basics of AI is one thing, but applying it to your business is a whole different ball game. It's like purchasing a high-performance sports car but not having the right roads or driving skills to make use of its full potential. The same goes for AI— without the correct infrastructure and cybersecurity measures, you won't be able to optimally utilize its capabilities.

## Chapter 8.1: Creating Spaces for Intelligence: Infrastructure and Cybersecurity for AI in Business

As the founder of a promising start-up, Amelia was thrilled by the prospect of integrating AI into her business operations. She had learned about AI's potential to streamline processes and improve decision-making. It all seemed like an exciting journey until she encountered an unexpected hurdle: Her current business infrastructure wasn't equipped to support AI.

Realizing the need for an upgrade, she consulted with experts who introduced her to two primary options: cloud-based and on-premise infrastructure. After careful consideration, Amelia chose a cloud-based solution due to its scalability, accessibility, and cost-effectiveness.

However, the move to a more sophisticated platform came with its own set of challenges: cybersecurity threats that could jeopardize both her valuable data and customer information. Amelia knew she needed robust security measures in place before fully embracing AI in her business.

Like Amelia, many businesses embarking on their AI journey must consider their existing infrastructure's adequacy and prioritize cybersecurity. This chapter aims to guide you through these crucial aspects of introducing AI into your business.

## Infrastructure for AI: Cloud Versus On Premises

To effectively implement AI in your business operations, having robust infrastructure is paramount. Two primary types dominate today's market: cloud-based and on-premise solutions.

Here is another example. I was talking with an old friend who had become a successful business owner, heavily relying on modern technologies such as artificial intelligence. As we reminisced about the past, our conversation naturally shifted to his experiences in implementing AI. What struck me wasn't just how he managed to deploy AI-driven solutions successfully, but the way he decided what kind of infrastructure and security measures were required for his AI implementation.

He started by telling me about his initial struggles in deciding between cloud-based infrastructure and on-premise deployment. He noticed that when he tried running simple machine learning algorithms on his existing servers, they would often crash or run unbearably slowly. That's when it dawned upon him—if you want to dabble into AI, you need robust hardware that can handle processing large amounts of data rapidly.

He initially opted for a cloud-based solution since it provided high scalability without any upfront investment in physical infrastructure. He chose a top-notch provider who specialized in managing AI-powered applications and could provide him with the necessary resources whenever needed.

But then a stark realization hit him: If he continued using cloud services for all his data storage and computing needs, wouldn't that expose his precious data to potential cybersecurity risks? After all, isn't it easier for hackers to access data stored on shared servers rather than private ones?

This made him reevaluate his decision. He began investing in building an on-premise setup while maintaining stringent cybersecurity protocols such as firewalls and intrusion detection systems. But even then, he didn't fully abandon the cloud, instead opting for a hybrid model where sensitive data remained onsite while less critical information resided in the cloud.

Cloud-based platforms offer flexibility, scalability, and accessibility from anywhere with an internet connection. They are ideal for businesses seeking cost-effective solutions as they eliminate the need for substantial upfront investments in hardware.

On-premise solutions provide control over your data since it is stored within your premises. However, they require substantial capital investment in hardware acquisition and maintenance.

In a research paper published by Gartner Research & Advisory Services titled *Comparing Cloud vs. On-Premises* (Moore, 2019), it was stated that "By 2025, 80% of enterprises will have shut down their traditional data center." This prediction highlights the growing trend towards cloud-based solutions driven by factors such as cost-effectiveness and scalability.

Several of the studies conducted by McKinsey Global Institute have highlighted how companies investing significantly in cloud-based systems showed higher profit margins compared to those sticking to traditional methods—demonstrating clearly why embracing change becomes paramount, especially when dealing with artificial intelligence.

## Securing Your Investment: The Importance of Cybersecurity

With increased reliance on digital platforms comes the risk of cyber threats. Protecting your valuable information becomes critical when adopting advanced technologies like AI.

A study conducted by IBM in 2023 found that "The average total cost of a data breach is $3.86 million." This alarming figure underscores how costly inadequate cybersecurity can be for businesses.

### *The Bottom Line: Prioritizing Infrastructure Upgrade and Cybersecurity*

Embracing AI requires careful planning around infrastructure upgrade choices between cloud or on-premise solutions based on your specific needs while also ensuring robust cybersecurity measures are put into place.

Cybersecurity measures should cover all areas vulnerable to attack, from securing network connections to protecting sensitive customer information stored in databases.

It's not just about safeguarding valuable data, but also demonstrating responsibility towards securing customer information—a factor that can significantly impact trust levels among customers and lead to greater brand loyalty.

Understanding your infrastructural requirements is not just about choosing between different types of setups, either. It's more importantly about understanding where your organization stands today and where you want it to reach tomorrow.

## Chapter 8.2: The Power of AI Incorporated With Edge Computing

You're standing on a precipice. In front of you is a vast landscape of potential, ripe for exploration and ready to be harnessed. It's called edge computing, and it's one of the most exciting developments in AI today. This chapter will guide you through its intricacies, helping you understand what it is, why it matters, and how it can transform your business.

If AI were a city, edge computing would be its infrastructure—roads, bridges, power grids—that makes things run smoothly behind the scenes. Essentially, edge computing refers to processing data near its source (the "edge") instead of sending it back to a centralized server or cloud for analysis. It's akin to having your own local supermarket instead of driving miles away just to buy groceries.

But why does this matter? Consider internet-of-things (IoT) devices like smart thermostats or wearable fitness trackers. These gadgets constantly produce data that needs quick processing for real-time feedback. Without edge computing, these devices would have to send all their information back to central servers for analysis before they could respond—think about receiving weather updates from your smartwatch only after a ten-minute wait.

Now, let's delve into some details.

Imagine running an autonomous vehicle company where each car generates terabytes of data per day—everything from road conditions and traffic patterns to pedestrian behavior. Sending all that information across long distances for processing not only slows down decision-making but also exposes sensitive information during transit—a cybersecurity nightmare!

Edge computing comes as a savior here by allowing each vehicle to process most data locally, right on board, while only transmitting necessary information—like crucial updates about mechanical issues or traffic incidents—back to home base, ensuring that it stays encrypted and secure.

Imagine a bustling factory where hundreds of IoT devices are at work, monitoring machinery, tracking inventory, and even predicting maintenance needs before they become critical. At the heart of it all is Layla, a tech-savvy operations manager who has successfully integrated AI and edge computing into her company's operations.

Under Layla's guidance, instead of sending vast quantities of data to a centralized cloud for processing—which could cause latency issues and consume significant bandwidth—the IoT devices process data locally. This edge computing approach speeds up response times, enhances data security, and reduces strain on network resources.

Just like Layla's factory, many businesses worldwide can benefit from deploying AI-powered IoT devices combined with edge computing. This chapter will guide you in understanding these advanced topics and offer practical advice on how to leverage them strategically in your business.

## Understanding the Role of the Internet in AI Functionality

The internet plays an indispensable role in artificial intelligence functionality. It provides the means for AI systems to access the vast amounts of data required for machine learning processes. Additionally, it enables real-time communication between AI systems and users or other systems across vast distances.

However, as businesses increasingly deploy thousands or even millions of IoT devices that constantly generate data, relying solely on centralized cloud-based processing becomes impractical due to latency issues and bandwidth consumption. This is where edge computing comes into play.

## Edge Computing: Bringing AI Closer to the Data Source

In essence, edge computing involves bringing computation closer to the source of data generation—for instance, IoT devices deployed onsite within a business environment such as Layla's factory. Doing so significantly reduces latency problems, as there's no need to send data over long distances to a centralized server for processing.

According to research by Gartner, Inc., "By 2022, more than 50% of enterprise-generated data will be created and processed outside traditional centralized data centers or clouds" (Moore, 2019). This shift underscores how essential edge computing is becoming in managing IoT device-generated data effectively.

To further prove this point, let's look at more evidence from the research conducted by Gartner, Inc., which predicted in 2018 that around 10% of enterprise-generated data was created and processed outside traditional centralized cloud-based systems; however, this number is set to rise up to 75% by 2025, showcasing the growing importance of edge computing in connection to IoT devices and AI functionalities.

For example, consider Amazon Go stores, which use combination sensors and cameras to track what customers pick up and put down in the aisles, eliminating the need for checkout lines because all processing is done locally within the store. Implementing edge-computing technology greatly reduced the time shoppers spend shopping, improving overall the customer experience significantly.

"To get ahead in life," Richard Branson once said, "one must take opportunities as they come." The same holds true in business, with new developments like edge computing offering opportunities worth seizing upon.

## Practical Applications of Edge Computing With AI

Consider smart security cameras deployed across your business premises. These cameras capture video footage 24/7, but not all this footage contains useful information. With edge computing coupled with on-device machine learning algorithms, these cameras can analyze footage locally in real time, deciding whether there's any unusual or suspicious activity worth flagging to human operators or not. This selective analysis greatly reduces unnecessary network traffic while enhancing security responses through quicker detection times.

It isn't just about speed, though; privacy protection is another crucial benefit offered by edge computing when integrated with AI functionalities on IoT devices. With edge computing, sensitive information doesn't have to leave local networks unless necessary, reducing potential exposure risks.

## The Bottom Line: Realizing the Synergy Between AI and Edge Computing

An astute business leader looking ahead into future trends should consider harnessing the synergy between artificial intelligence and edge computing within their organizations' operations. As businesses continue generating increasing volumes of valuable data via IoT devices every day, it becomes mission-critical that this wealth of information is processed efficiently and securely without causing an excessive drain on network resources.

Embracing this powerful combination will allow your business not only keep pace with technological advancements, but also achieve peak operational efficiencies, enhance service delivery, ensure robust cybersecurity measures are in place—and, more importantly, deliver value-added experiences to customers, thereby staying competitive in a dynamic marketplace.

Analyzing these examples shows us two things: First, how crucial a role edge computing plays in ensuring smooth operation and efficient functioning of IoT devices; and, secondly, that edge computing has the potential to significantly improve user experiences across various sectors, for businesses large and small alike.

A case study published by IEEE Professional Communication Society explores the use of edge-computing in the telecommunication industry. Operators deploying mobile networks found significant reduction in costs associated with transferring large amounts of data long distances. More importantly, they improved customer satisfaction due to the lower latencies and faster network speeds achieved through localized processing techniques involved in edge computing.

So, how can you leverage this powerful tool? Well, firstly, start identifying areas within your organization that could benefit from quicker response times. Then look into possible solutions available, and ensure they are suited to the market and the specific needs of your business. Lastly, ensure proper training so that staff know how to handle new systems effectively—avoid any potential mishaps due to lack of knowledge or skill.

In conclusion, embracing innovative technologies acts like a catalyst, propelling your business forward in the digital age and providing a competitive advantage to those willing to adapt. With ever-increasing volumes of data generated every day, it's becoming imperative that businesses adopt smarter ways of managing and analyzing orders to stay ahead of the curve. So, next time you find yourself standing on the precipice of change, remember that sometimes the best view comes after the hardest climb.

# CHAPTER 9:
# FUTURE TRENDS AND PREDICTIONS
# IN AI TECHNOLOGY

Sophia, a humanoid robot designed by Hanson Robotics, was unveiled to the world in 2016. She could hold conversations, recognize faces, understand speech, and even express emotions through various facial expressions. Sophia was not just a showcase of how far artificial intelligence had come, but also an indication of the potential it held for the future.

As we delve deeper into this chapter, we'll explore the trends and predictions surrounding AI technology that could revolutionize your business operations.

## Predicted Increase in AI Adoption

AI's adoption rate is predicted to skyrocket as more businesses realize its potential to enhance productivity and efficiency. According to PwC's Global Digital IQ Survey (*How can organisations reshape business strategy with AI?*, n.d.), "54% of executives plan to implement AI solutions within their organizations."

Start by identifying areas where AI can streamline your operations. It could be improving customer service through chatbots or improving supply chain management using predictive analytics. The possibilities are endless.

## Enhanced Customer Relations With AI

In an era where customer experience is king, businesses must stay ahead of customer expectations. Here's where AI comes into play.

AI can analyze vast amounts of data from different touchpoints, helping you understand customers' behaviors and preferences on a granular level. This insight can then be used to deliver personalized experiences that exceed expectations.

According to Salesforce Research's *State of the Connected Customer* report, "84% of customers say being treated like a person is very important to winning their business." AI enables just that—personalization at scale (Afshar, 2018).

## Sales Growth Through Predictive Analysis

Predictive analysis uses historical data combined with machine learning algorithms to forecast future outcomes accurately. For sales teams, this means predicting which leads are most likely to convert or what products will sell best during specific seasons.

AI's ability to sift through complex datasets quickly makes it instrumental in enhancing sales performance.

## Improved Employee Satisfaction

While there's fear about job losses due to automation driven by AI, the reality might be less ominous. Automation could take over mundane tasks, allowing employees more time for strategic and creative roles, leading to higher job satisfaction levels.

## *The Bottom Line: Embracing the Future*

As you navigate through an evolving digital landscape, incorporating artificial intelligence into your business strategy isn't just advisable; it's crucial.

It's not only about leveraging technology for growth but also building a resilient organization capable of tackling future challenges head-on.

AI isn't science fiction anymore—it's happening right now, with companies investing billions into Neurolink technologies aiming at integrating human brains with computers seamlessly—an extension of AI capabilities beyond our wildest dreams!

But that's not all. Imagine walking into stores where there are no cashiers or salespeople but rather robots guiding you through aisles based on your preferences saved from past shopping experiences—or automated vehicles navigating traffic while you catch up on emails or read a book during your commute—all powered by advanced AI systems.

By visualizing these scenarios, you're turning knobs and immersing yourself in this futuristic world ruled by AI and recognizing its immense potential. It is not just for convenience but also for increasing productivity, reducing errors, and saving valuable time.

As we shift towards this reality, it's crucial for businesses to invest in understanding and adopting AI solutions not merely as tools but as integral components driving their growth strategy. They must adapt or risk becoming obsolete in this fast-paced tech-driven world.

So remember as you step into tomorrow that, with every tap on your smart devices, you're partaking in shaping that exciting future with AI.

The key takeaway here is seeing beyond our present situation and understanding how advancements in artificial intelligence can revolutionize our lives—in ways we might never have imagined before. Embracing change rather than fearing it is critical if we want to keep pace with technological progress and harness its full potential for better living standards and business success.

# CHAPTER 10:
# THE ROADMAP TO IMPLEMENTING AI
# IN YOUR BUSINESS

Once upon a time, there was a local pizza joint called "Papa Luigi's," known for their delicious pizzas and friendly staff. However, they struggled with managing the influx of orders during peak hours and often ended up with unhappy customers due to delayed deliveries.

The owner, Luigi, thought about how he could streamline his business operations and enhance customer experience. After doing some research, he decided to implement an AI system to manage orders and deliveries more effectively.

Within months of implementing the AI system, Papa Luigi's saw significant improvements in their service. Orders were handled efficiently, and delivery routes were optimized, leading to quicker deliveries and ultimately happier customers.

Much like Luigi's pizzeria, your business can also benefit from implementing AI into its operations. This chapter will guide you through understanding the potential of AI for your business needs and provide step-by-step advice on how to integrate it seamlessly into your operations.

Another example: I was having a conversation with a business owner who had successfully integrated artificial intelligence (AI into his operations. He ran an e-commerce company, and in the early stages, their customer service department was overwhelmed with queries. He could have hired more staff to manage this, but instead, he turned to AI. He implemented a chatbot system on his website that could handle basic inquiries from customers.

This may sound simple enough, but what struck me about this businessman's approach wasn't just the fact that he used AI—it was how he decided which part of his operation needed it the most.

Incorporating AI into your business is not just about replacing humans with robots or software; it's about identifying areas in your organization that can benefit from automation or intelligent analysis. Think about mundane jobs that are necessary but time-consuming; these are your "knob-turners." In direct-response marketing terms, these areas were like those customers who walked up to the TV set and started turning knobs—they showed potential for conversion.

Before diving headfirst into AI implementation, it's essential to understand what aspects of your business can benefit from AI. Is it customer service? Operations? Marketing? Identify areas where efficiency can be improved or tasks that can be automated.

*Companies that have designed an AI strategy that aligns with their organizational goals are twice as likely to obtain benefits from AI implementation.*
–McKinsey & Company study, *The State of AI in 2020*

We'll begin our journey by identifying where we are now and deciding on our destination.

### Step 1: Understand Your Current Position

Like setting off on any journey, before implementing AI into your business processes, it's essential first to evaluate what technology infrastructure is already in place. What data do you have available? How digitally mature is your organization?

## Step 2: Define Your Destination

Next, define what success looks like for you. Do you want AI to help automate repetitive tasks? Or perhaps employ predictive analytics for better decision-making? Clearly defining what you hope to achieve using AI will guide the direction of this implementation process.

## Step 3: Choose the Right Vehicle

Not all cars are suitable for every road trip; similarly, not all types of AI applications might be right for your specific needs. In such scenarios, bringing in third-party experts who specialize in deciphering which type of AI technology would best for your specific needs is invaluable during this process, as they can offer unbiased advice based on experience across various sectors.

## Step 4: Assemble Your Crew

Integrating new technology is not just about the systems; your employees are key players in this transformative journey. Engage them early and often throughout this process. Provide training programs so they can skill up and adapt comfortably to these changes. It's crucial that they understand why you are implementing this change and how it will help them rather than replace them.

Training sessions should be held so employees can learn how to work alongside these new digital colleagues effectively. Remember, employees who feel involved in the process are more likely to embrace change.

The enemy here isn't change itself, but resistance against it—a common pitfall many organizations fall victim to when implementing new technology such as AI.

*Key Idea From This Chapter: Implementing artificial intelligence isn't about replacing human effort; it's about augmenting it— freeing up time and resources so that humans can focus on higher-value tasks.*

Now, let's talk about roadblocks! Like any long drive, there may be obstacles along the way—technical glitches and employee resistance being two common ones. Here's what you do if things get particularly tough:

If the problem lies within technical challenges, consider seeking additional support from external tech consultants or vendors specializing in these areas.

If employee resistance becomes a hurdle, invest time in explaining why these changes are necessary and beneficial both at an organizational and individual level.

Remember, it's okay if progress seems slow initially; even small steps forward count!

Implementing AI doesn't necessarily mean needing vast amounts of additional physical space, but you need to ensure there is enough digital space for storing data securely. Planning out data storage requirements in advance is key for successful implementation without a hitch.

## The Bottom Line: Achieving Successful AI Adoption

The key takeaways here are simple:

• Before embarking upon the "AI journey," understand where you currently stand technologically.

- Define clear objectives regarding what exactly you hope to achieve using artificial intelligence.

- Not every type of AI application might be suitable for your particular needs; choose wisely.

- Engage employees throughout this process—they're key contributors towards successful implementation.

- If faced with significant challenges during implementation, consider seeking external help.

- Be patient. The path towards successful AI integration might seem slow initially, but perseverance pays off.

By following these steps as outlined above—much like Luigi did with his pizzeria—you too will reap the benefits offered by integrating artificial intelligence into your business operations.

# CONCLUSION:
# MAKING AN INFORMED DECISION
# ABOUT AI

Imagine a company called TechCo, struggling to keep up with their competitors. Their customer service was slow and inefficient, they were losing track of their inventory, and worst of all, they were wasting precious time on tasks that could have been automated. Then they discovered artificial intelligence.

After implementing an AI solution, TechCo's customer service became faster and more accurate due to the introduction of an AI-powered chatbot. Their inventory management system was updated in real time thanks to AI algorithms, eliminating errors and reducing expenses. Mundane tasks were being performed by AI software, freeing up valuable time for the employees.

The transformation at TechCo brought to the forefront the potential of AI for businesses everywhere. This chapter will guide you on how to make an informed decision about whether AI is right for your business.

## Understanding How Other Businesses Benefit from AI

Many businesses have seen significant growth after implementing AI solutions into their operations. For example, Amazon uses AI for product recommendations, while Netflix leverages it for personalized streaming suggestions.

According to multiple reports by McKinsey Global Institute, AI adoption outside of the tech sector is just beginning, but can significantly boost profits for firms who embrace the technology (Balakrishnan et al., 2020; Bughin et al., 2018). Given these facts, it's worth considering how your own business could benefit from adopting similar strategies.

### Evaluating if Artificial Intelligence Is Right for Your Business

Before deciding whether or not to implement artificial intelligence solutions in your company, assess your current operational pain points. Are there repetitive tasks that consume much of your employees' time? Do you need better insights from your data? Could your customer service be enhanced?

AI offers solutions for all these issues and more; hence, identifying such areas can help you decide if it's right for you.

### Analyzing What Artificial Intelligence Can Do for Your Business

An essential aspect of this decision-making process is understanding what precisely artificial intelligence can do for your business. From improving efficiency through automation and enhancing customer service with chatbots or virtual assistants to providing deeper insights with predictive analytics, the possibilities are endless.

A study by Accenture (2017) revealed that "businesses who apply AI could increase profitability by an average of 38 percent by 2035." This clearly shows that investing in artificial intelligence can offer substantial returns in the long run.

### *The Bottom Line: Deciding Whether to Implement Artificial Intelligence*

Deciding whether or not to incorporate artificial intelligence into your business strategy is a significant step forward. It requires a thorough understanding of what AI has to offer and how it aligns with your business goals.

Once implemented correctly, though, as TechCo experienced firsthand, the benefits are transformative.

With this knowledge at hand from this book and beyond, you are now equipped to make an informed decision about whether or not artificial intelligence is the right fit for your business.

# REFERENCES

A. M. Turing. (1950). Computing Machinery and Intelligence. *Mind 49:* 433-460.

Accenture. (2017, June 21). *Accenture Report: Artificial Intelligence Has Potential to Increase Corporate Profitability in 16 Industries by an Average of 38 Percent by 2035.* Accenture Newsroom. https://newsroom.accenture.com/news/accenture-report-artificial-intelligence-has-potential-to-increase-corporate-profitability-in-16-industries-by-an-average-of-38-percent-by-2035.htm

Accenture Interactive. (2018). *Making it personal: 2018 personalization pulse check.* Accenture. https://www.accenture.com/_acnmedia/pdf-77/accenture-pulse-survey.pdf

Afshar, V. (2018, June 5). *State of the connected consumer report: New research uncovers big shifts in customer expectations and trust.* SalesForce. https://www.salesforce.com/blog/digital-customers-research-blog/

*Albert Einstein quotes.* (n.d.). BrainyQuote. brainyquote.com/quotes/albert_einstein_148778

*Albert Einstein quotes.* (n.d.). Goodreads. https://www.goodreads.com/quotes/556030-imagination-is-more-important-than-knowledge-for-knowledge-is-limited

*Albert Einstein quotes.* (n.d.) Goodreads.
https://www.goodreads.com/quotes/1799-the-world-as-we-
have-created-it-is-a-process

Autor, D. H. (2016, August 15). *The shifts—great and small—in
workplace automation.* MIT Sloan Management Review.
https://sloanreview.mit.edu/article/the-shifts-great-and-small-
in-workplace-automation/

Balakrishnan, T., Chui, M., Hall, B., Burkhardt, R., & Henke, N.
(2020, November 17). *McKinsey Global Survey: The state of AI in
2020.* McKinsey & Company.
https://www.mckinsey.com/capabilities/quantumblack/our-
insights/global-survey-the-state-of-ai-in-2020

BCG. (n.d.). *Personalization (in marketing and sales).* Boston
Consulting Group. https://www.bcg.com/capabilities/marketing-
sales/personalization

Benjamin, G., Brink, H., Camara, T., Egleston, E., Faucher, J.,
Gilson, K., Kadyan, A., Kervazo, F., Lavandier, H., Masri, K., May,
B., Muthiah, S., Naucler, T., Prema, M., Raghubanshi, V.,
Rieniets, S., Sarda, K., Surak, Z., & Vivek, K. (2020, February). *The
productivity imperative in services.* McKinsey & Company.
https://www.mckinsey.com/~/media/mckinsey/business%20fun
ctions/operations/our%20insights/the%20productivity%20imper
ative%20in%20services/the-productivity-imperative-in-
services.pdf

Berg, A., Bounader, L., Gueorguiev, N., Miyamoto, H., Moriyama,
K., Nakatani, R., & Zanna, L.-F. (2021, July 16). *For the benefit of
all: fiscal policies and equity-efficiency trade-offs in the age of
automation.* IMF Working Papers.
https://www.imf.org/en/Publications/WP/Issues/2021/07/16/F

or-the-Benefit-of-All-Fiscal-Policies-and-Equity-Efficiency-Trade-offs-in-the-Age-of-462133

Bhowmik, A. (2023, May 13). *Sundar Pichai says AI will 'touch everything': 'every sector, every industry, every aspect of our lives'.* Benzinga. https://www.benzinga.com/news/23/05/32378624/sundar-pichai-says-ai-will-touch-everything-every-sector-every-industry-every-aspect-of-our-lives

Brown, B., Kanagasabai, K., Pant, P., & Pinto, G. S. (2017, March 15). *Capturing value from your customer data.* QuantumBlack AI by McKinsey. https://www.mckinsey.com/capabilities/quantumblack/our-insights/capturing-value-from-your-customer-data

Bughin, J., Seong, J., Manyika, J., Michael Chui, M., & Joshi, R. (2018, September 4). *Notes from the AI frontier: Modeling the impact of AI on the world economy.* McKinsey Global Institute; McKinsey & Company. https://www.mckinsey.com/featured-insights/artificial-intelligence/notes-from-the-ai-frontier-modeling-the-impact-of-ai-on-the-world-economy

Buvat, J., Yardi, A., Girard, S., Taylor, M., Thieullent, A.-L., Gadri, G., Sengupta, A., & Khemka, Y. (2018). *The secret to winning customers' hearts with artificial intelligence: Add human intelligence.* Capgemini Research Institute. https://www.capgemini.com/wp-content/uploads/2018/07/AI-in-CX-Report_Digital.pdf

Cattell, J., Chilukuri, S., & Levy, M. (2013, April 1). *How big data can revolutionize pharmaceutical R&D.* McKinsey & Company. https://www.mckinsey.com/industries/life-sciences/our-insights/how-big-data-can-revolutionize-pharmaceutical-r-and-d

Chaubard, F., Fang, M., Genthial, G., Mundra, R., & Socher, R. (2019). *CS224n: Natural Language Processing with Deep Learning* [Lecture Notes: Part 1]. Stanford University. https://web.stanford.edu/class/cs224n/readings/cs224n-2019-notes01-wordvecs1.pdf

Crawford, K. (2021). *Atlas Of AI.* Yale University Press.

Davenport, T. H., and Ronanki, R. (2017, January). *Artificial intelligence for the real world.* Harvard Business Review. https://hbr.org/2018/01/artificial-intelligence-for-the-real-world

DDSN Interactive. (2021, January 15). *Bill Gates.* https://ddsn.com/blog/digital-design-service-technology-quotes/bill-gates.html

Dhingra, N., Samo, A., Schaninger, B., & Schrimper, M. (2021, April 5). *Help your employees find purpose—or watch them leave.* McKinsey & Company. https://www.mckinsey.com/capabilities/people-and-organizational-performance/our-insights/help-your-employees-find-purpose-or-watch-them-leave

*Enhancing business performance with AI solution integration: A deep dive.* (2023, May 2). Exlns AI. https://www.exlns.ai/blog-detail/enhancing-business-performance-with-ai-solution-integration-a-deep-dive

Epsilon. (2018, January 9). *New Epsilon research indicates 80% of consumers are more likely to make a purchase when brands offer personalized experiences.* https://www.epsilon.com/us/about-us/pressroom/new-epsilon-research-indicates-80-of-consumers-are-more-likely-to-make-a-purchase-when-brands-offer-personalized-experiences

Fontanella, C. (2022, September 13). *14 customer loyalty trends to follow in 2022*. HubSpot, Inc. https://blog.hubspot.com/service/customer-loyalty-trends#:~:text=HubSpot%20found%20that%2090%25%20of,as%2010%20minutes%20or%20less

Ganesh, K. (2023, August 2). E*mployee engagement and change management: How are they connected.* CultureMonkey. https://www.culturemonkey.io/employee-engagement/employee-engagement-and-change-management/#:~:text=Engaging%20employees%20in%20the%20process%20by%20involving%20them%20in%20decision,personally%20committed%20to%20and%20engaged

*How can organisations reshape business strategy with AI?*. (n.d.). PwC. https://www.pwc.com/gx/en/issues/data-and-analytics/artificial-intelligence/organisations-business-strategy.html#:~:text=54%25%20of%20executives%20say%20that,intelligence%20to%20strengthen%20human%20decisions

IBM. (2023). *Cost of a Data Breach Report 2023.* https://www.ibm.com/reports/data-breach

Janegar, R. (n.d.). *Data is the new oil.* The Commerce Society; Shri Ram College of Commerce. https://comsocsrcc.com/data-is-the-new-oil/

Johnson, K. B., Wei, W., Weeraratne, D., Frisse, M. E., Misulis, K., Rhee, K., Zhao, J., & Snowdon, J. L. (2020). Precision Medicine, AI, and the Future of Personalized Health Care. *Clinical and Translational Science, 14*(1). https://doi.org/10.1111/cts.12884

Kubota, T. (2017, November 15). *Stanford algorithm can diagnose pneumonia better than radiologists.* Stanford News. https://news.stanford.edu/2017/11/15/algorithm-outperforms-radiologists-diagnosing-pneumonia/

Lynch, S. (2017, March 11). *Andrew Ng: Why AI is the new electricity.* Insights by Stanford Business. https://www.gsb.stanford.edu/insights/andrew-ng-why-ai-new-electricity

McGilvrey, J. (n.d.). *Creative Web Design: How to Harness the Power of Visual Storytelling.* Jeremy McGilvrey Web Design Agency. https://www.jeremymcgilvrey.com/creative-web-design

McKinsey Global Institute. (2017, January). *A future that works: automation, employment, and productivity.* McKinsey & Company. https://www.mckinsey.com/~/media/mckinsey/featured%20insights/Digital%20Disruption/Harnessing%20automation%20for%20a%20future%20that%20works/MGI-A-future-that-works-Executive-summary.ashx#:~:text=While%20less%20than%205%20percent,than%20will%20be%20automated%20away

McKinsey Global Institute. (2017, June). *Artificial intelligence: the next digital frontier?.* McKinsey & Company. https://www.mckinsey.com/~/media/mckinsey/industries/advanced%20electronics/our%20insights/how%20artificial%20intelligence%20can%20deliver%20real%20value%20to%20companies/mgi-artificial-intelligence-discussion-paper.ashx

Mitchell, T. M. (1997). Machine learning. Mcgraw Hill.

Moore, S. (2019, August 5). *The data center is (almost) dead.* Gartner. https://www.gartner.com/smarterwithgartner/the-data-center-is-almost-dead

Moore, S. (2022, February 9). *Gartner says more than half of enterprise IT spending in key market segments will shift to the cloud by 2025.* Gartner (via Stamford Connection).

https://www.gartner.com/en/newsroom/press-releases/2022-02-09-gartner-says-more-than-half-of-enterprise-it-spending

Mubarak, Y., & Koeshidayatullah, A. (2023). Hierarchical automated machine learning (AutoML) for advanced unconventional reservoir characterization. *Scientific Reports*, 13(1), 13812. https://doi.org/10.1038/s41598-023-40904-0

Nadella, S. (2021, August 11). *Digital ecosystems point the way to the future.* Robert Bosch GmbH. https://www.bosch.com/stories/digital-ecosystems/

Ng, A. (2013, March). *Machine learning and AI via brain simulations* [PowerPoint Slides]. Stanford University. https://ai.stanford.edu/~ang/slides/DeepLearning-Mar2013.pptx

Orr, L. M., & Orr, D. J. (2014). *Eliminating Waste in Business.* Berkeley, CA Apress.

Parichay Brand Consultants. (2016, September 27). *Customer service is the new marketing. - Derek Sivers.* LinkedIn Pulse. https://www.linkedin.com/pulse/customer-service-new-marketing-derek-sivers-founder-parichay/

Perry, C. (2011, October 18). *You're not so anonymous.* The Harvard Gazette. https://news.harvard.edu/gazette/story/2011/10/youre-not-so-anonymous/

Priest, M. (2023, May 12). *Conversational AI market outlook - updated 2023.* Boost.AI. https://www.boost.ai/blog/conversational-ai-market-outlook#:~:text=Gartner%20predicts%20that%20by%202022,ha ve%20relied%20on%20for%20years

Quiseng, B. (n.d.). *Guest blog: Don't confuse customer services with customer service*. Shep Hyken; Shepard Presentations, LLC. https://hyken.com/customer-loyalty/guest-blog-dont-confuse-customer-services-with-customer-service/

*Robin Sharma quotes*. (n.d.). Goodreads. https://www.goodreads.com/quotes/8598941-change-is-hard-at-first-messy-in-the-middle-and-gorgeous

Sawers, P. (2019, June 14). *Google's chief decision scientist: Humans can fix AI's shortcomings*. VentureBeat. https://venturebeat.com/ai/googles-chief-decision-scientist-humans-can-fix-ais-shortcomings/

Shah, M. (2022, March 26). *A person who never made a mistake never tried anything new*. SetQuotes. https://www.setquotes.com/a-person-who-never-made-a-mistake-never-tried-anything-new-albert-einstein/

Stancombe, C., Thieullent, A.-L., KVJ, S., Chandna, A., Tolido, R., Buvat, J., & Khadikar, A.. (2017). *Turning AI into concrete value: the successful implementers' toolkit*. Capgemini Consulting; Digital Transformation Institute. https://www.capgemini.com/consulting-de/wp-content/uploads/sites/32/2017/09/artificial-intelligence-report.pdf

Stanford Online. (2023, May 11). *Andrew Ng and Fei-Fei Li Discuss Human-Centered Artificial Intelligence - Stanford Online* [Video]. YouTube. https://www.youtube.com/watch?v=UNhC6Ox0T0o

*Steve Jobs quotes*. (n.d.). BrainyQuote. https://www.brainyquote.com/quotes/steve_jobs_173474

Sundstrom, A. (2023, March 12). *The global chatbot market size is projected to surpass around USD 42 billion by 2032.* LinkedIn Pulse. https://www.linkedin.com/pulse/global-chatbot-market-size-projected-surpass-around-usd-sundstrom/

*20th CEO Survey.* (2017, January). PwC. https://www.pwc.com/gx/en/ceo-survey/2017/deep-dives/ceo-survey-global-talent.pdf

Verweij, G. & Rao, A. S. (2017). *Sizing the prize: What's the real value of AI for your business and how can you capitalise?.* PwC. https://www.pwc.com/gx/en/issues/analytics/assets/pwc-ai-analysis-sizing-the-prize-report.pdf